What people are saying about

Living Fairy

There's a big movement toward the re-wilding of the natural environment these days. In *Pagan Portals: Living Fairy*, Morgan Daimler aims to re-wild the spiritual world as well. From historical sources to personal experience to detailed rituals, Daimler offers tools for calling the Fairy Folk and related beings back into our world. This is not a book of twee fairies with shimmering wands and sparkling dust, but a deep exploration of ancient Powers that were once part of our world but were driven out by religious and cultural forces. This book aims to help them return to their rightful place.

Laura Perry, author of *Ariadne's Thread: Awakening the Wonders of the Ancient Minoans in Our Modern Lives* and founder of Modern Minoan Paganism

While I'm an initiate of a different fairy ˙   ˙ition... Anderson Faery...and I'm not any kind ⸀   ˥en, some of what is said about the Pleiʔ   ˌh lore passed down to me as part of   ˌuch of it parallels my own simplified ˙   ˌe. It echoes as well my long-held convictꞮ   ˌerworld used to be more in alignment with ours,   ˌs fallen out of that alignment, and that the shift back intꞮ   ˌance is both something that is happening and needs to be encouraged to happen. Where will it all lead? I don't know. But I find the fact that Morgain Daimler and I, as well as some others, seem to be converging on something from different directions both exciting and faintly alarming. Which is usually what happens when Those Folks are involved. If you're interested in wild, old, deep things, and can handle the feeling you get when you suddenly realize you're no longer sure where you are, read this book. And then go time your witchcraft by the stars.

Sara Amis, author of *A Word to the Witch* and columnist for *Witches & Pagans* magazine

Brilliant! Morgan Daimler once again brings us back to the magick of the Faeries. She takes us deeper into the practice of Faery Witchcraft that connects us to the Otherworld and the power of the stars. Through her practice and experience, she weaves the magical thread that connects us to Faery magick of the past with the the celestial fabric of the Pleiades in the night sky. This book is a fantastic tome that teaches how to connect with the Faery powers in a deep and meaningful way. This is a must have for anyone seeking to build their relationship with the Faeries and develop their spiritual practice.

Chris Allaun, author of *Underworld: Shamanism, Myth, and Magick* and *Upperworld: Shamansim and Magick of the Celestial Realm*

The experience of reading Daimler's book is rather like being taken firmly by the hand and danced through a whirlwind tour of both historical fairylore and the author's own lived experiences and hard-won gnosis. From academic perspectives and informed theories to pragmatic advice and practical rituals, *Pagan Portals: Living Fairy* provides a desperately-needed guidebook to the realities of working with the Good People, written by one of the foremost modern practitioners at the intersection of witchcraft and the Fairy Faith.

Misha Magdalene, author of *Outside the Charmed Circle: Exploring Gender & Sexuality in Magical Practice*

Pagan Portals

Living Fairy

Fairy Witchcraft and Star Worship

Pagan Portals

Living Fairy

Fairy Witchcraft and Star Worship

Morgan Daimler

MOON
BOOKS

Winchester, UK
Washington, USA

JOHN HUNT PUBLISHING

First published by Moon Books, 2020
Moon Books is an imprint of John Hunt Publishing Ltd., No. 3 East Street, Alresford
Hampshire SO24 9EE, UK
office@jhpbooks.net
www.johnhuntpublishing.com
www.moon-books.net

For distributor details and how to order please visit the 'Ordering' section on our website.

Text copyright: Morgan Daimler 2019

ISBN: 978 1 78904 539 0
978 1 78904 540 6 (ebook)
Library of Congress Control Number: 2019953033

A CIP catalogue record for this book is available from the British Library.

Design: Stuart Davies

UK: Printed and bound by CPI Group (UK) Ltd, Croydon, CR0 4YY
US: Printed and bound by Thomson-Shore, 7300 West Joy Road, Dexter, MI 48130

We operate a distinctive and ethical publishing philosophy in
all areas of our business, from our global network of authors to
production and worldwide distribution.

Contents

Other Titles by Morgan Daimler

A New Dictionary of Fairies

A 21st Century Exploration of Celtic and Related Western European Fairies

978-1-78904-036-4 (paperback)

978-1-78904-037-1 (e-book)

Fairies

A Guide to the Celtic Fair Folk

978-1-78279-650-3 (paperback)

978-1-78279-696-1 (e-book)

Fairycraft

Following the Path of Fairy Witchcraft

978-1-78535-051-1 (paperback)

978-1-78535-052-8 (e-book)

Fairy Queens

Meeting the Queens of the Otherworld

978-1-78535-833-3 (paperback)

978-1-78535-842-5 (e-book)

Fairy Witchcraft

A Neopagan's Guide to the Celtic Fairy Faith

978-1-78279-343-4 (paperback)

978-1-78279-344-1 (e-book)

Travelling the Fairy Path

Experiencing the myth, magic, and mysticism of Fairy Witchcraft

978-1-78535-752-7 (paperback)

978-1-78535-753-4 (e-book)

Dedicated to everyone who has been following along with me on this journey. This book would never have happened without your encouragement.

Special thanks to Mel, Cat, and Nicole for crashing that troll party with me, which started all of this Pleiades stuff to begin with. Extra thanks to Seo Helrune for all the helpful discussions.

Dangerous Things - A Poem

I may be cynical
but I have earned it
so I laugh
I do
when I hear people
talking about
the Good People
being drawn by wind chimes
and shiny baubles
although I probably said
much the same once myself.
I shake my head
at the idea
that They wish us
nothing but well.
Cynical, yes
sharp as a thorn prick
coated in blood
sharp as salt heavy
on the tongue
sharp as the longing
for an Saol Eile.
They have never been
safe
and people forget that
at their own peril
It is always
degrees of risk
My life used to be
my own
before the rath

before the cave
before the fire on the hill
My hair used to be straight
My heart used to be whole
People can keep
their windchimes and baubles
their human made 'elf-locks'
misnamed madness
their wishful thinking
I will tell you plainly
wishes are dangerous things

Author's Note

This book is the result of a paradigm shift that occurred for me in Iceland in 2018 and the way that shift has rippled through my life since then. It is also proof that no matter how long we experience the Otherworld and its inhabitants or how long we follow a given spirituality there is always room for change and growth.

I have been an Irish-focused pagan since 1991 following a path based on neopagan witchcraft and the Fairy Faith. In the last three years my focus has shifted more fully to the Daoine Maithe and an emphasis on early modern witchcraft but the core of my spirituality stays the same. After writing my last book in the Fairy Witchcraft series – 'Travelling the Fairy Path' - I didn't plan to write anything further on the subject. However, as things have continued to evolve for me, I have shared that journey, especially my experiences crafting holy days connecting the fairies to the Pleiades, online and there was a lot of interest in that material being available as a book. This book is the result.

My usual caveat to readers: in writing this I have drawn on many different sources and have carefully referenced and cited all of them. My own degree is in psychology so I prefer to use the APA method of citations. This means that within the text after quotes or paraphrased material the reader will see a set of parentheses containing the author's last name and date the source was published; this can then be cross references with the bibliography at the end of the book. I find this method to be a good one and I prefer it over footnotes or other methods of citation which is why it's the one I use. I have also included end notes in some places where a point needs to be expanded on or further discussed but where it would be awkward to do that within the text itself.

This book is written for those who follow a specific form

of Fairy Witchcraft but I hope it will also be of use to others outside that niche. This book grew from a conversation with my friend Seo Helrune – who is a big part of almost everything in the following text – about the idea of re-enchanting the mortal world. It's a concept that has been coming up in the last few years among different communities and one I have written about myself. It is the core of this book and the reason it came to be written. My view has always been that to achieve this re-enchantment of our world we need only to change how we perceive it because there is plenty of enchantment already here. But experiences in Iceland in September 2018 have changed my understanding of several things including this subject. I believe now that it is essential that we do actively seek to bring the Other into our world and that it is essential for us to return our world to a state of balance with the Otherworld by opening the way for it again.

Morgan, October, 2019

Introduction

Calling The Othercrowd Back

"And see not ye that bonny road,
That winds about the fernie brae?
That is the road to fair Elfland,
Where thou and I this night maun gae."
Thomas the Rhymer, traditional Ballad

There is something shifting between the human world and the Otherworld, something that has been shifting for several years now. Some balance that had once been achieved and had existed for a very long time has been lost or disrupted. This feels very jarring to us, enough that I know many people sensitive to these things who have been disturbed by the palpable shifting, but I suspect it may be a return to a state that existed millennia ago and which the Othercrowd seeks to establish again. Our Western world is out of alignment with these energies and these beings in ways that other parts of the human world which haven't alienated and driven out their Others aren't. Perhaps it was inevitable then that the pendulum must swing back the other way. The question for us then, as witches who have any connection to the Good Folk, is what we should do.

Much of our out-of-sync-ness now with the Otherworld is a direct result of Christian, particularly Protestant, efforts to drive out the Good Neighbors who they believed were demons. There are deep implications in this for those of us who live in Christian held lands. If we are in places where the dominant religion has been and may still be actively working to drive out the spirits that we in turn are allied with, what does that mean for us?

There's abundant evidence that some Christian traditions did indeed view the Othercrowd as demonic and classified them as demons; we see as much in witchcraft trial accounts where a person who spoke of fairy familiars and dealing with the Queen of Elfame was described by judges as dealing with devils and Satan. There are many examples where terms like elf or goblin are glossed as imp or incubus, going back at least to the 15th century in England and found in the American colonies from their inception.

Related to this is a pervasive campaign of propaganda saying that priests and other such religious men had driven out the Good People through their faith, despite continuous anecdotes and folklore to the contrary. One can argue that these stories of the religious men forcing out the fairies is another means to try to affect their removal by weakening people's belief in them and removing the power of folkloric stories tying fairies to places, as well as eroding practices designed to honor them.

For example, Chaucer's Canterbury Tales, 'the Wife of Bath's Tale' 14th century:

"In the days of King Arthur, Britain was full of fairies. The elf queen danced in meadows with her companions. This is what I read, anyway. Now, no one sees elves any more, because of the prayers of friars. These friars search all over the land, blessing every building and house, with the result that there are no more fairies. Where elves used to walk, the friar himself now goes at all times of the day, saying his prayers. Women can walk anywhere they want without fearing anyone but the friar, who will only dishonor them, rather than beget demon children upon them."

In Bishop Richard Corbet's 16th century poem 'Farewell, Rewards, and Fairies' he says that the fairies tolerated Catholics well enough but have all fled to other lands to get away from Protestant religion, which is why none can now be found. In a similar vein several anecdotes beginning in the 17th century mention fairies fleeing any area where church bells rang, apparently unable to tolerate the sound (Briggs, 1976).

Perhaps we can still see echoes of this effort today not only in the disenchantment of the world and the places where the spirits have in fact been driven off but also in the wider cultural views that see the world around us as un-inspirited and empty. In the way that the dominant narrative may try to describe all things within their own cosmology only as if there could be no other possible options.

So, getting back to my earlier question - for those of us who operate in a very different paradigm and for whom interacting with Otherworldly spirits, or any spirits really, is an intrinsic aspect of what we do, how do we respond to this?

I think we fight back. I think we fight fire with fire, propaganda with propaganda. We spread our own stories and our own truth and talk about the reality of the spirits that are there in defiance of that dominant narrative. And if they call them demons then let them call them demons. I think we look at the world around us and see it as it is, alive and inspirited, and we learn to be aware if we aren't already of the Othercrowd when they are around us. But most essentially like repairing a rip in a tapestry I think we must actively work to fix what's been done over the centuries; as Seo Helrune put it in the article 'Restoration Not Re-enchantment', we restore the Othercrowd to their place in our world. And yes, they can be and often are dangerous; so are wolves and bears and poisonous snakes but our world needs those as well.

I believe we need to restore the balance that was by returning things to the way they used to be when the world was full of Otherworldly spirits. And I think we can do this. We can call them back. We can reopen the old pathways. We can re-find the old practices and ways. We can re-align ourselves with the Good Neighbours and restore the balance by undoing what the Protestant Church did when they drove those beings out. It won't be safe but it is essential.

Chapter 1

Going Deeper

"Here is no protective circle, no prayers, no names of power; we have left the strained company of the magicians and are back in the countryside where the fairies are natural company."
K. Briggs, 'The Anatomy of Puck'

The beginning of calling the Othercrowd back for me was going much deeper with my own witchcraft and spiritual practices. This has been multilayered, and I won't tell other people what they should or shouldn't do here because I know that this type of practice isn't for everyone. What I will do is take a look at some of the complicated history that exists between witches and the Good People. The reader can decide for themselves if there are aspects of this that perhaps apply to themselves or might be beneficial in their own lives.

There is a long history of witches working with fairies in various ways, both learning from them and being in service to them. In modern paganism we more often see this relationship played out very differently, with the Good Folk being approached from a more ceremonial magic perspective or treated as a kind of spirit guide or friend. When we look to folklore and early modern witchcraft, which may reflect at least a shadow of the original relationship, we see a different picture and it is this one that I base my own personal practice on and which I think can help create a stronger connection with them.

There are accounts from the Scottish witchcraft trials where accused witches talk about encountering fairies, or even of fairies seeking them out, and offering to teach them and work with them if the human would make an oath to the Queen of fairy or her representative. This oath was nothing to be taken lightly but was a serious pledge to the Queen that involved renouncing one's previous faith and exchanging it for loyalty to the monarch of the Otherworld. The Queen might then give the human witch a fairy familiar[1] which was a fairy who would act as a go-between for the witch and the fairies in general.

The witch would be expected to come when summoned to attend gatherings of the fairy Queen's Court and would be taught by her or the familiar, some of them earning great renown as cunningfolk from these teachings, and in some cases being given other things as well. This was not a thing done by the human's will or choice but was something that happened instead when the fairies reached out and directly engaged with a person on their own terms. The dynamics of this engagement then are very different from what we see in the grimoire tradition where a fairy might be invoked much as any other spirit could be using a precise ritual format and for the human's purpose.

When a human, witch or magician, is the one in control the situation is of course very much different although one might argue no less risky. The risk involved is simply of another nature. There is a corpus of grimoire material that deals with conjuring and commanding fairies, which is part of what Briggs was referring to in the opening quote of this chapter, and these rituals include specific suggestions for how to invoke and bind fairies. There are also hints in some of the ballad material, like the ballad of Tam Lin, that a compass (circle) of holy water will protect a person inside it from the Good Neighbours indicating another means by which a person might use ritual to insulate themselves from the fairies. For those seeking to call the Othercrowd up and command them or bind them, protection is certainly an essential component as they will not be pleased when they arrive.

And therein lies the crux of the difference between the two approaches and why perhaps we see the idea of more ritualized work with fairies requiring protective spaces and names of power while more intuitive approaches do not. To use a compass is to be in control; to walk without one is to acknowledge that you aren't in control. This is wild witchcraft that walks through the dark woods and knows that all life is both beautiful and precarious. It is a path that one walks without any assurance of safety and sometimes without any clarity on where exactly the path is leading. Sometimes there isn't even a path to follow, just trees and darkness. But it is a witchcraft that is full of wonderful and uncanny things and for people who are drawn to it, it is a witchcraft that feels alive and inspired.

I opened this section with a quote from Katherine Briggs because I feel that it perfectly sums up the dichotomy that exists among people who deal with fairies. There are those who approach them with protective circles, prayers, and names designed to control and there are those who approach them without those things, but perhaps with an offering and a good word. How they are approached sets the tone for the entire relationship that may follow, and it is understandable that many would rather choose to control the situation than risk being controlled by it. But when you are in control you will only ever gain as much as you can bargain for, and with Themselves that will never be as much as you think it is. When you are willing to turn yourself over to them – and I don't discount exactly what that means or why the Church saw it as the same thing as selling your soul to the Devil – then you will gain as much as they are willing to give you. And they will always freely give more than they ever will give by compulsion.

Let us look then at what exactly we are getting into when we plunge deeper into this connection. In this section I am going to share a collection of my personal experiences, some good and some bad, that have come from my own deeper work with these beings. As we strive to bring this energy more fully into the human world we should – perhaps must – be aware that the affects will be both beneficial and detrimental. Move forward with your eyes open, as it were.

There are many good things that come from connecting to and working with (in any sense) these beings. These good things can take a variety of forms and may be things that impact a person in deeply private ways or that are expressed in ways that other people also perceive. They may be minor things that are nonetheless valuable or major things that are vital. There is an old and longstanding taboo against bragging too much about fairy blessings in your life and so one must always be cautious about what and how much they talk about, but generally speaking anything that other people were also involved in or aware of is safe to share. Why this prohibition? I have a couple ideas but I suspect the main reason is simply that it keeps us from taking these blessings for granted. That said here are three good things that being connected to the fairies has meant for my life.

They've guided me when I was physically lost – kind of the opposite of being pixy-led, there have been a few times when I've lost my way in an unfamiliar place and the Good People have helped me find where I needed to be again. In one case driving in a car with two other people late at night in a strange city we took a wrong turn and ended up very lost (this was back before GPS); I started seeing a form in front of us and instructed the driver where to turn to follow it. We ended up back where we needed to be within about five minutes. Another time, when I was in Ireland, I wandered off from the group I was with and got turned around in a field. I couldn't see anyone else from the group, it was starting to get dark, and I had no idea where I was. I made an offering and was guided back to the main pathway and a friendly (human) face.

They saved my life – several years ago I had a severe anaphylactic reaction. It was late at night and even though I knew what was happening I was frightened enough that I was in denial and decided if I just went to sleep everything would be alright. Lying there with my tongue swelling and having trouble breathing, my husband was suddenly and somewhat violently awakened by what he described later as a 'large moth'[2] flying into his face, causing him to get up and turn the lights on. There was no moth to be found anywhere but at that point I broke down and asked him to call an ambulance.

They saved my house from a fire – I was sitting in my living room and kept seeing movement near the outlet by our television. I initially dismissed it, acknowledging that it was fairy activity (which I can see) but not concerned. I was getting ready to leave to run an errand but kept getting distracted by this movement and finally when I thought I saw a small figure walking in that area I walked over to see what was going on. As I got within a few feet of the wall the cord plugged into the top outlet sparked and then started burning; because I was so close, I quickly pulled it out before the wall caught fire.

Along with the good things that have come from working with the Fair Folk there have been bad things, although I will admit the bad is often (not always) my own fault. Generally, when a negative thing occurs it is a result of me transgressing an etiquette rule, pushing a taboo, or ignoring directives which are part of my spiritual work. Occasionally however negative things are simply a result of being in the wrong place at the wrong time, which is a risk of doing this kind of work. I also want to be clear that when I say 'bad' I mean bad consequences that result directly from some aspect of this work, rather than difficult things like those aforementioned prohibitions which are certainly also a factor but which I wouldn't categorize as bad per se.

As with the previous examples I'm going to offer three, and you'll notice several of them are medical; in those cases, yes, I sought professional medical help and no the situation couldn't really be explained by doctors. These may sound a bit extreme but these did all really happen and I'm sharing them in part to illustrate what I mean by bad. It's important to be aware that this work can have real physical consequences.

They interfered with my eyesight – just prior to a trip to Ireland in 2018 I was working to get a manuscript finished, which I wanted to have done before I left. In the two weeks prior to the trip I started having dreams and otherwise receiving messages that I should stop working on the project and start focusing on the Gentry and on getting ready for some intense spiritual work that would be going on. Being stubborn I didn't want to listen so I kept pushing, knowing I could get the book done before I left if I put the effort in. After a few days of this I developed a strange eye infection that caused blurred vision – meaning I couldn't type or be on the computer very much because I couldn't see – and which the doctors and ophthalmologist couldn't explain. They diagnosed it as a bacterial infection of 'unknown origin' and gave me some ointment to put in my eyes. Once I stopped trying to get any work done and started focusing on the spiritual things my vision cleared up.

They drained my car battery – I have a specific personal prohibition relating to my spiritual work. One of these has some layers to it, and I was skirting around part of it to visit a cemetery with my children. I had a bad feeling about the whole thing and suspected that I was edging into doing something I shouldn't. When I went to park my car, I had a very strong sense not to turn the car off or get out myself but I did anyway. Walking back up to the car afterwards I knew it wouldn't start, and it didn't. So, I was stuck with three very upset children in a cemetery in the woods, with an hour wait for roadside assistance. Despite trying multiple times to start the car it was clear the battery was dead. It was very hot, the children were upset and thirsty, and the situation was a lot more unstable than I can easily put into words. Finally, I had a talk with my Otherworldly people and basically said if they would let the car start, I wouldn't make the same mistake again (and I'd drive directly to get a new battery for the car). The car then started immediately. I'll probably never hear the end of this incident from my kids.

I was sick for about six months – this one may have been kind of inevitable as an after effect of an initiatory experience I went through involving the Good Neighbours in Ireland, but afterwards I was inexplicably very sick for about six months. I went to the local walk-in clinic and saw my primary care several times and was told it was everything from lingering viral bronchitis to possible repetitive walking pneumonia, but nothing helped it and no one could explain why I wasn't getting better. I was just sick and stayed sick from Samhain until Bealtaine. This was, at the least, a very difficult experience to go through connected to this spiritual work.

Not everyone who decides to connect with the Good Folk will end up with this level of engagement, which is fine. Like any other type of witchcraft or spirit work there's a range of interaction that occurs and for some people this will mean minimal but safer encounters while for others the work will be deeper and more dangerous. At least speaking for the kind of Otherworldly beings I deal with danger and blessing are two sides of one coin and the more dedicated you are to fairy work the more you are open to both. It's good to keep this in mind if you are considering this path in any serious way. There will be positive things that come your way but there will also be equivalent levels of risk and potential negative experiences. If this is a path that interests you, you should go into it prepared for both the good and the bad. It is also something to think about as we seek to bring the Other more fully present into our world. We may perhaps be making things less safe for ourselves but we are certainly making our world much fuller in the process.

Some Words of Caution

I know I say this often and if you have read my previous books this won't be new to you but as we plunge into the idea of restoring the Other to the human world I think it's important to review some points that may be difficulties or confusions.

Some of these may seem obvious or self-evident but they are all things I have run across, more than once, from various people. Clearly those people would disagree with what I'm about to say. This can be understood as my personal opinion based on my own study and experience, but I stand by them.

If you want to incorporate the Good People into your pagan or witchcraft practice, here's some things to keep in mind:

Lack of Boundaries - This is an important one. Many, many people seem to approach dealing with the Fair Folk as if they are harmless, kind, higher beings[3] who only mean us well and therefore should be given carte blanche in a person's life. And I'm sure there are certain types of spirits and even some kinds of fairies that do fall into the 'harmless and helpful' category. But not all of them by far. And it is really dangerous to just offer a blanket invitation to anything and everything Otherworldly because you think they won't hurt you and are all sweetness and light - or they won't hurt you because you are a witch and that somehow offers you special protection. It doesn't. Boundaries and warding are not only your friend but are absolutely essential. Especially as the presence of the Othercrowd increases in the human world.

However tempted you are to just freely invite in anything you perceive as a fairy because it's a fairy, don't do this. At the least treat them like you would a human being, with appropriate caution until you have a sense of who and what they are.

Tunnel Vision – It's easy to get tunnel vision and assume our own cultural experiences or viewpoint are universal when they aren't. Part of understanding the current shift in Otherworldly energy, in my opinion, is understanding how our cultures and areas got to the state of imbalance we are in and looking to other places on earth that never developed such an unhealthy relationship to their spirits is key for comparison. Part of that is understanding that what we for convenience call the Fairy

Faith isn't a worldwide phenomenon although there are similar practices elsewhere, and that animism is found across the globe. If we look to places that still have a healthier relationship with their Other spirits, we can learn a lot about what that should look like, and we can also see the ways that our own places are out of sync.

We Don't Worship Fairies - We may worship deities associated with Fairy, including the Tuatha De Danann who are also said to be Kings and Queens of Fairy hills, but we don't worship fairies in general. I think part of this confusion may come in because we do offer things to them and give them a reverential respect. Or atavistic fear. We offer to them to keep on their good side and to avert potential harm. We offer to them not because we worship them but because they are owed a portion of the harvest, and also it's a pretty effective way to appease anything that's annoyed. We respect them because they can and will impact our lives for good or ill if we don't. But we don't worship them the way other religions worship Gods. It's a nuance but it's an important one.

Fairies Aren't...A Lot Of The Things People Say They Are - There's massive confusion about what the Good Folk are, which is fair because it's a confusing subject. I mention this because I see a lot of people who try to incorporate fairies into their practice by pigeonholing them into a specific narrow category, usually nature spirits, elementals, or some kind of earth angel. This is really problematic because then the person moves forward as if all fairies are only and entirely that narrow thing. Which of course they aren't. So, another big tip to moving forward in creating a deeper practice with the Good Folk is acknowledging the diversity and that while you personally may only or by preference interact with a small specific group there is actually a lot of other possibilities out there.

We Don't Rule Over Them – Listen, I'm just going to be blunt here I am immediately skeptical anytime I see a person claiming to be in a position of power over the Good People. Especially if its implied that position is based on caretaking in some sense. They don't need us to care for them. The meme that goes around in December talking about Christmas trees being based in a tradition of bringing a tree in to give a forest spirit a warm place in the cold is nonsense. The people who talk about being in charge of fairies in a certain place or of leading a group of fairies? I'm not buying it. There are methods based in ceremonial magic to command, compel, or bind fairies that's true but that doesn't grant a human rank or inherent authority over the Fair Folk. There are also cases of humans with fairy familiars but again the human doesn't have authority over that being - in fact usually the fairy was assigned to the human by the Fairy Queen and one might argue they are there in part to keep an eye on the human.

Respect Matters - Probably tied into most of the other points above, but another big mistake I see many people making is a simple lack of respect. The majority of these beings aren't twee 20th century flower fairies or the goofy fairies found in modern kids TV shows. These are beings who have been shown a level of respect for thousands of years because they can seriously mess a human up. They won't all do that and some kinds are more benign than others as was mentioned but many can and will bring illness, madness, maiming, or death sometimes for no other reason that it amuses them to. Take the Slua Sidhe for one example of that. If you want to interact with these beings safely on any level then respect is vital. Even if you feel like you have a group you deal with that is of the small harmless sort don't forget they aren't all like that and don't let your guard down or drop the company manners.

Effort Matters Too - Far too many people jump into fairywork with no deeper knowledge about fairies than the plot of their favourite young adult novel or game and they never go any further. They treat it all like a game as well, making things up as they go along based on what they personally like or feel like doing. The truth is if you, as a pagan or witch, want to seriously get into this it is going to take some effort. There are good books and blogs out there to be found (avoid any that hit on the points already mentioned) and there are good YouTube videos and podcasts. If you are going to get into this any deeper than knowing what to do and not to do to keep from getting maimed then you are going to have to put effort in. Lots of effort. There's no other way.

Well, that's some of my cautions and suggestions anyway. Do with them as you will. I hope that this chapter has provided some food for thought about the idea of deeper practice and also potential consequences of doing so.

End Notes

1   This is a complicated subject in itself. All I'll say here is fairy familiars were sometimes dead humans who seemed to have been taken by the fairies and usually had a connection to the witch, perhaps as a blood relative. In other cases, they are beings entirely of Fairy.

2   I have a strong personal connection between moths and the Gentry and have had other experiences linking them; interestingly Grimm in Teutonic Mythology also connects moths and butterflies to elves.

3   I'm not going to compare them to angels here because I read the Bible and angels are really scary.

Chapter 2

In Practice

"Then he went on, and on, and on, till he came to the round green
hill with the terrace-rings from top to bottom, and he went round it
three times, "widershins", saying each time:
"Open, door! open, door!
And let me come in."
And the third time the door did open, and he went in"
Childe Rowland

As we move forward into a restored world there are a few
particular aspects of witchcraft practice I'd like to discuss that
are essential but also vary from mainstream neopaganism. The
first two cover topics that are often neglected on the one hand or
overdone on the other: cleansing and casting a compass or circle.
Cleansing or purifying yourself, energy, and places is something
that should be done regularly especially as we work towards
this restored connection between worlds. On the other hand, the
usual approach to ritual space, whether we call that casting a
compass or circle, may need to be rethought or changed to be
more in line with a different focus. Both of these topics should
be given some serious thought as they relate to how we interact
with the energy around us and of the Otherworld. Bridging from
that we will discuss the idea of a spirituality that isn't deity
centered but based around spirits that are not gods, per se.

Purification and Cleansing of Baneful Energy

The idea that the world contains both energy that is beneficial
to people and should be encouraged and energy that is harmful
to people and should be protected against or cleansed from
people seems to be fairly ubiquitous across cultures. My own

understanding of this subject is largely based on my study of pre-Christian Ireland and more modern Irish folklore. Many aspects of how the pre-Christian Irish pagans specifically would have viewed this concept and dealt with it has been lost, of course, but hints remain and these hints as well as modern folk practices are more than enough for a person to create a viable system to work with today. When we look at the Iron Age Irish, we mostly find the idea of what harms people embodied as spirits and so we see means to fight or drive off these spirits. We also find the idea that people through their actions can place themselves into or out of human society with people outside of society having a distinct and dangerous energy to them that must be purified before they return to civilization. Interestingly it is often these people outside 'civilization' that seem to be most appealing to the Good Folk.

We can find a few hints in mythology and ritual practices that indicate that people who intentionally stepped outside of society needed to be ritually cleansed before re-entering it. Specifically, there is indications that a person who had left society to live in a wild state and who wished to re-enter society needed to be ceremonially cleansed using a process that featured a ritual meal, usually a broth (McCone, 1990). This process may have involved the broth being both consumed as well as asperged over the person or symbolically bathed in. This broth would have been made from food that was being offered to the Gods and so was sacred by association as it were. The Fianna, who lived a portion of their time outside society, seem to have had cleansing rituals in order to re-enter society later and these rituals may have involved ritual anointing with milk or butter (PSVL, 2011). In this way we see that the food used for ritual feasting could play a role in purification, particularly the more significant or serious purifications including redeeming people who had been living wild or as outlaws.

On a simpler level we see the concept of entering a sacred

place or space, especially for ritual or magical purposes, by first walking three times around the space deiseal [clockwise]. This practice has remained through the modern period in folk practices, but the concept of approaching somewhere from a sunwise direction with positive intentions, or indeed circling it against the sun for cursing, can be found in the mythology indicating the deep roots of the idea. It is a quick and basic way to draw beneficial energy, to simply walk clockwise around something.

As with many other cultures we also see the idea of burning different herbs to cleanse away baneful energy. The most well known in Irish and also Scottish culture may be juniper, which is mentioned by various authors, including Danaher, Evans, and MacNeil, for its protective qualities in folk belief and for the widespread practice of burning juniper in the home and stables on the Quarter (Scottish cross-Quarter) days to be rid of dangerous energy and to bless the space and people. Another less well-known herb burned for protection against evil spirits and baneful magic was mugwort, which was also kept around the home, tied onto livestock, and worn on a person's clothing for purification and to ward off fairies and witches (MacCoitir, 2006). Rosemary was also used especially as a fumigant in sick rooms, carrying the idea of cleansing away lingering illness or baneful energy in the atmosphere. For our purposes all three of these should be used in different contexts, with Mugwort considered particularly for use driving out dangerous spirits.

Maintaining a good habit of purification and cleansing is essential. Perhaps especially so for those who seek to walk a liminal way or who intentionally step outside society's bounds on a regular basis. The more baneful or harmful energy you may be around the more important it is to make sure you purify and cleanse often, but even if you live within society and keep on the straight and narrow (as it were) it's a good idea to at least purify and cleanse on the major holidays. I recommend a combination of the above-mentioned methods, although I favor incorporating moving sunwise (or depending on circumstance against the sun) into everything you do, with intention.

Fairy Witchcraft Circles

Modern witchcraft, be it neopagan or trad craft, utilize compasses or circles[1] for various reasons and in slightly different ways, but ultimately often using a very similar framework. While it's entirely possible to use variations of any of these in a witchcraft aimed more directly at interacting with fairies there are also other options. I'd like to explore that here, and also discuss my own current approach to the practice.

My understanding is that circles in ceremonial magic were used to protect the magician from whatever they were summoning. In modern neopagan witchcraft the most common explanation I've seen for their use is to contain energy that's raised, and secondarily to protect those within from outside forces. There're many ways to create these barriers, but the basic approach is to face each cardinal direction, one at a time, and invoke the spirit of that direction then walk the boundary of your circle visualizing an energetic barrier forming. For traditional witches casting a compass is done differently, although the general concept is still the same, and the purpose is to separate the space from the mundane.

All of these are good practices within their respective traditions or spiritualities which is why they exist as traditions. When I started out in witchcraft, I believed they were more than just good, I thought they were essential. But I started to realize that most of the time there just wasn't any need to go to the trouble to cast a full circle/compass. It was tradition for the sake of tradition rather than for a real purpose.

There is a lot of evidence of circles in folklore and early modern witchcraft, but probably not what you're imagining. If we're not looking at the ceremonial material – arguably often the work of the elite rather than the common practitioner – we don't find complex rituals or exotic ingredients. What we do find in most cases is simply walking in a specific direction to circle an area for a purpose. In Ireland and Scotland there's evidence of movement deiseal [clockwise] done for blessing, usually three times, and movement tuathail [counterclockwise] done for malediction. Moving in a circle might be done to take an oath, break a spell, or cast enchantments or protective magics (Wimberly, 1928). The movement and the direction were equally important.

If we look at the ballad material, we can find an example that might be closer to the idea of a witches' circle, but again not the modern one. In some versions of the Ballad of Tam Lin the variously-named protagonist uses holy water to cast a compass around herself, apparently so that she will remain unseen by the Fairy Rade:

"There's holy water in her hand,
She casts a compass round,
And presently a fairy band
Comes riding o'er the mound."
(Tam Lin 39D)

Generally, the protagonist takes this action after being explicitly told to by her fairy lover:

"You'll go down to Mile Course,
Between twelve o'clock and one,
And fill your hands with holy water,
And cast your compass round"
(Tam-a-Line 39G, modified to English from the original Scots)

In this case the circle of holy water acts as a protection for the woman from the fairies who are passing by and keeps her hidden from their sight until she moves outside the circle's bounds. This is particularly noteworthy for us as we look to shaping our own practices.

In modern witchcraft moving in a circle tuathail is often viewed as either connected to negative magic or to undoing something; for example, some traditions go counterclockwise to take down a circle that's been cast. In the older material while it is true that this direction of motion is associated with cursing it is also connected to Fairy. In the Ballad of Childe Rowland the protagonist's sister is taken into Fairy after going around a church widdershins [counterclockwise], with the implication that this action opened her up to fairy abduction; in the same way to gain entrance to rescue her the protagonist must walk three times round widdershins himself. In some of the Scottish witchcraft trial accounts the accused witches said they would turn or circle widdershins a certain number of times when seeing the new moon or meeting their patron (the Devil or the Queen of Fairy). Circling tuathail then is more nuanced than simply baneful magic, and I have found its very useful in my own practices.

My current approach is heavily influenced by early modern witchcraft and folk practices, which means the sources I look to include the ones I just discussed above. There's no focus there on formal, multi-step circle casting – things are done by walking with intention or perhaps by sprinkling some holy water or milk[2] as you walk. The direction you walk in is important but each direction, with or against the sun, has its uses. I tend to see walking deiseal as blessing and walking tuathail as a means to connect to Fairy, although cursing is also a use for that movement. Sometimes my entire ritual might consist of nothing but moving with intention in a particular direction. You might be surprised how powerful walking or dancing in a particular direction while singing can be (or you won't be surprised if you've done it before).

I write about an option in my book 'Fairy Witchcraft' to cast a more formal circle whose purpose, as in traditional witchcraft, is to separate the area from the rest of the world. Specifically, the idea is to use the circle to open a pathway to Fairy, although I admit this isn't something I often use formal ritual to do. I included it in the book to give people that framework if they need it, but for myself at this point I usually just stick with walking tuathail and chanting. For people moving deeper into these practices or who have experience with this type of witchcraft I would encourage some experimenting with this to see how you feel about a less formal method yourself.

In full ritual if I use a compass, I cast it with clean water, blessed by me in the name of the Powers I serve. I sprinkle the water as I walk and I ask that that space be purified and be opened to the spirits I am working with. It's not fancy and it's not complicated but it's effective. I only do this in situations with the sorts of Fairy beings who have higher standards for the spaces they occupy and who I wouldn't invite into an area that wasn't fit for them. In most smaller rituals or works of magic I don't use compasses at all because they haven't proved necessary.

In many areas of paganism and witchcraft some form of circle casting will be found as standard operating procedure for rituals, but often the reason why this is done every time didn't make sense to me or didn't make sense with what I was doing. I've never done well with practices I've been expected to do by rote without a solid understanding of why, and so I found that when I dug into why I was supposed to be casting a circle in ritual or magic most of the reasons didn't gel with what I personally did. It wasn't until I researched back and found the older types of circles that I found practices that resonated with me and which I understood intuitively. Then I shaped my own practice from there, with years of trial and error to figure out what did and didn't work and what was and wasn't essential.

Water and walking are as formal as I need to get, and it works just as well – better for me personally – than anything else I've ever tried. And as I work to nurture this deeper connection to the Otherworld, I have found that simpler is more conducive not less.

Pagan Witchcraft That Isn't Deity Focused

For the majority of the time I've been a pagan I had been fairly deity focused as that's just the template that paganism in the United States tends to go by: almost everything from magical practices to celebrations involve deity one way or another. However, things changed profoundly for me in October of 2016 and that change began a shift away from the Gods we find in mythology and into a clear focus on the Othercrowd. While I don't believe this sort of shift is for everyone or will occur to everyone, and while I do also discuss connecting to Liminal Gods who are relational to Fairy, I think it's important here to explore the value of a witchcraft that isn't deity focused.

As I've gravitated more towards primarily focusing on the Daoine Maithe (fairies) and as my previous ties to specific deities have fallen away my practice has changed significantly if slowly. So, what follows is my own answer to the question of what non-deity centred pagan witchcraft can look like, with an understanding that different people may have very different understandings and approaches to this.

What Is a God Anyway? One of the first challenges in answering a question about non-deity centric pagan witchcraft practice is understanding how I define what a god. Maybe that seems like an easy question, but I don't think it is; and in fairness some of the beings that I do honour as higher powers might be considered deities by other people. My own approach for a long time has been to use a sort of sliding scale based on power and ability to influence the world, with the very bottom end including beings that are very limited in what they can do and affect and the top including beings that have a great deal of influence which I might label as gods. I have never viewed deity – any deity – as omniscient, omnipotent, or omnipresent though so the top end of the scale while far, far beyond human ability is still limited in some ways. Perhaps not many, but some.

A secondary criterion I use, which is more straightforward and less subjective, is whether a being has historically been understood or worshipped as a deity. So obviously personages like Odin, the Morrigan, Hecate, Isis, Ares, and so on fall into the deity category without my worrying about where they fall on my personal scale of power. If a previous or existing culture viewed a being as a deity I'm not going to argue.

Where it gets very fuzzy is when there's not a lot of historic material (or none) or we are trying to decide where the line is between a deity, a Fairy Queen, and a very powerful spirit. I'm currently in a place where I hesitate slightly to call the main Powers I deal with deities because they, themselves, don't seem very fond of that terminology. I have referred to them as Liminal Gods because that's the easiest way to convey their overall position in the scheme of things but often the concepts are fluid and unclear. I could as easily say they are Queens and Kings of Fairy groups, with a nod to the muddled connection between gods and Fairy monarchy. I suppose the short answer is they seem to prefer Fairy Queen or King to God and I just go with that. Clear as mud? Yeah.

Beyond that though the main beings I actually, practically, engage with aren't on that high end of the power spectrum. My daily life, for the most part, isn't about Gods by any name or guise but about the spirits that are around me and who I have built connections with. When I talk about my Heathenry, as I practice it, might best be described as Alfatru because my specific focus on and belief in the Huldufolk is the cornerstone of my Norse spirituality. I can say the same thing about my Irish spirituality and my focus on the Daoine Maithe, although with the Aos Sidhe it is by nature more complicated and convoluted.

Either way though it is these in-between beings, perhaps not Gods[3] but definitely powerful and able to influence the world around me that are my main focus.

So, how do I craft a paganism that is about these spirits and not the gods? Honestly it seems pretty straightforward to me. My daily and weekly practice involves looking at strengthening and maintaining the connections I have with these Otherworldly beings and with the spirits in the world around me. I pay a lot of attention to spirits of the land and of my home, to make sure everything is as it should be. I listen to them and try to respect what they might need in a given circumstance, and ultimately at the least I try to be a good neighbour to them as much as I'd like for them to be to me[4]. The bulk of my witchcraft and my spirituality is based on these connections and on the beings that I find the most present.

On holy days, which I admit are in flux for me right now and which we'll discuss in depth in chapter 5, I focus on the wider cycle being celebrated and, on the spirits, (daoine maithe, huldufolk, specific beings) connected to that time. I may invite them to join me in my celebration or ritual, depending on what kind of spirits we're talking about, and I may make offerings for them. My approach to offerings is that the Good People are owed them as much or perhaps more than the gods may be and also that giving to them as seasonal points builds luck and success.

In my magical work my focus is on nurturing alliances and friendships with Otherworldly beings, rather than calling on deities. In situations where I would need to appeal to a higher power as authority to intervene on my behalf – perhaps when I'm trying to deal with a dangerous spirit for example – I would call on the Fairy Queen I am connected to. Similarly, while I don't pray often right now when I do, I pray to the liminal Gods or Fairy Queen, or look to the more powerful spirits I deal with. It is like a web of symbiotic connections built on interaction and offering.

One thing that's important to understand in all of this is that it very much isn't about an either/or mindset. I'm not denying the Gods or even choosing not to focus on them, and I am and do include them when it feels right or appropriate. I know they exist and that they are powerful and important beings. I have no qualms, unless I feel uncomfortable in a specific circumstance, about participating in deity-centric rituals. For me though the Gods, as generally defined and understood, are not where my own focus is. At least not on a daily basis. Kind of like I know that trains are important and exist but 99% of my life doesn't involve them in any significant way, even though they are vital to other people. Maybe one day that will change, because life is all about constant change, I don't know.

That's about where I'm at with my own spirituality and I hope that at least gives some idea of how I approach a non-deity based pagan witchcraft at this point. I suppose it may seem strange to some people, but if I'm being honest, I find the obsession with everything being so deeply deity based a bit odd myself. Even when I was including gods in my paganism it was always only a percentage of my focus, divided between gods, spirits, and ancestors. The gods are important but the spirits who are with us every day and whose places we interweave our own lives with seem a lot more immanently important in my opinion.

End Notes

1   the concepts of casting a circle or casting a compass are effectively synonymous, and in fact the term 'compas' or 'compasse' in Scots means "a round or ring; a circle or circuit". In practice they also seem to have many similarities, particularly the older versions.

2   Wimberly discusses the possible connection between the holy water used in Tam Lin and milk, and given the significance of milk it makes sense to me to use that as a substance to make a boundary holy.

3   nó b'fhéidir andéithe?

4   a little euphemistic humour, sorry I couldn't resist

Chapter 3

What Comes in Dreams

"The green hill cleaves, and forth, with a bound,
Comes elf and elfin steed;
The moon dives down in a golden cloud,
The stars grow dim with dread;
But a light is running along the earth,
So of heaven's they have no need:
O'er moor and moss with a shout they pass,
And the word is spur and speed"
The Faerie Oak of Corriewater

Dreams are a powerful avenue of communication between those in this world and those in the Otherworld, and it's always worth remembering that dreams should be considered as real when they involve the Othercrowd as any interaction in the waking world. Over the years I have gained a lot of knowledge from my dreams and messages or lessons communicated to me through them; in this chapter I would like to share several specific things that have come to me which I feel may be useful to anyone seeking a deeper journey with the Good Folk.

I can't always share the things I get in dreams, but when I can I do try to, not only so that other people can make use of them but also because I want to encourage other people to trust in what they might be getting in dreams or journeys. Use discernment and always double check any information you get especially relating to healing or herbs but don't be afraid to take information you get in dreams seriously. What follows is a selection of material that I am comfortable sharing here.

Cleansing

In one dream I was taught how to use various forms of peppermint for cleansing energetic attachments and spirits from a person. This is fairly straightforward and can be tailored to the person's circumstances but as with anything involving herbs please research the safety for yourself and also make sure any form is alright medically for to you to use.

Peppermint oil: rub on the pulse points and crown; alternately take a bath with a few drops of the oil and a bit of sea salt.

Peppermint (herb): drink in a tea three times a day for three days.

Peppermint (herb): burn to use as a fumigant around the afflicted person.

A Healing Charm

One night in 2018 I had a dream and was given this healing chant. This happened around 1 am and I woke up afterwards but as I was very tired, I didn't get up to write it down. I did remember it the next morning and had to try to figure out how to write it out properly. This was a bit more difficult than you might think because, as sometimes happens, it was given to me in modern Irish and while I have some modern Irish, I'm much better with old Irish. When I'm given things in modern Irish, I don't always know what all the words mean or how to write them out from hearing them spoken but can usually suss it all out afterwards[1]. I do this by writing it down based on my best guess for what I think it should be and then asking my friends who are Irish speakers to help me smooth it out. In this case the next day several people helped me with the spelling and grammar[2].

This is the healing chant as it was given to me:

"Gruaig le gruaig

craiceann le craiceann
cnámh le cnámh
feoil le feoil
fuil le fuil
casadh an chneá"

In English, roughly:

'hair with hair
skin with skin
bone with bone
flesh with flesh
blood with blood
turning/twisting the wound'

Anyone who wants to is welcome to make use of this. It's new as far as I know but it's similar in style to several other older healing chants for injuries, including, 'Charm of the Sprain' from the Carmina Gadelica and the Second Merseburg Incantation. It would be used by holding the hands over the injury and chanting the words three times.

Rabbit Bone Divination

In 2018 I started feeling a nudge to create my own divination system with bones. I was driving home and the idea came to me, and I tried to push it aside because it seemed too complicated for me to take on, but the idea just kept lingering. I kept getting the idea of using rabbit bones[3] for this purpose and it just wouldn't go from my mind. I finally asked for some kind of omen and as I crested a hill a wild rabbit hopped into the road in front of me; I slowed and the rabbit looked right at me before slowly hopping back the way he'd come. My feeling with this was that he was trying to get my attention, but I wasn't totally clear on the purpose so I risked asking for clarification - and turned a corner only to have a second wild rabbit run next to my car in someone's yard for about 30 feet before breaking off. To me this was a definitive sign that I should pursue this new divination method, even though I was very uncertain about how it would actually work.

I took a leap of faith and started moving forward with the project. I got a selection of ethically sourced small rabbit bones (from the feet) and I put them on my altar. I sat with them and meditated on how this should functionally work. My feeling was that it would be a system involving throwing bones down on a cloth, but nothing else was really coming to me for it. I decided that a good approach would be to ask for a bit of assistance. That night before I went to bed, I repeated three times:

> "*Coinín, coinín, coinín*
> *Speak to me truly*
> *Coinín, coinín, coinín*
> *Tell me what I need to know*"

I woke up with the image of bones being shaken and thrown down in my mind, and these words:

> "*One for fate*
> *Two for chance*
> *Three for loss*
> *Four for romance*
> *Five for life*
> *Six for death*
> *Seven for the Fair Folk*
> *Who steal your breath*
> *Eight for dark*
> *Nine for light*
> *Ten for aid*
> *Eleven for spite*

Twelve for health and
Blessings felt
Thirteen for fate
Yet undealt."

Each line, to me, represents a specific possible answer to a person's future although I also think this charm could have other uses[4]. What I gained from this was the idea to use thirteen bones and throw them down onto a small cloth marked with a circle and then look at how they fall and how many fall within the circle. I will chant the charm before I throw the bones.

Meditating on this later that day I also got the impression to burn one side of each bone, so that one side would be dark and the other plain. This could be used for yes/no questions or other points where clarification is needed as well as to indicate the overall tone of a result.

I am still developing this system and if anyone else chooses to try using it I encourage experimenting and working on your own approaches to it.

Cáca Síofra (Fairy Cake)

I have shared this before but because I mention it several times in chapter 5 as a recommended ritual offering, I want to include it here again. Also, it is another good example of something taught in a dream.

I had a dream one night and in the dream I was shown how to make little offering cakes for the Daoine Eile. I was shown through actions how to make them for the most part and the only thing I was told in words was the oat flour and the name of the cakes, so I'm guessing on the temperature and timing. If you try making them keep that in mind and adjust as necessary. Also, I don't bake (or cook particularly well) so bear with my terrible attempt to convey how to do this from what I saw in the dream. They didn't look like modern cakes but were denser and flatter.

Cáca Síofra:
3 eggs
1/2 cup honey
1/2 cup oat flour

Stir up eggs until blended then add in honey, then slowly add flour. Pour into buttered or greased cake pan or divide into several smaller ramekins[5]. Cook at about 350 degrees F (176 C) for about 35 - 40 minutes for cake, 30 minutes for larger ramekin, 20 minutes for smaller. Take out of oven when the center seems done. Drizzle more honey on the top when cooled.

I mentioned this on my social media the following morning and several people who actually can cook suggested cooking them on a griddle like pancakes. I've tried both ways, and am reporting the results below.

I tried them as griddle cakes and as little cakes in 2 sizes of ramekins. The batter is slightly thinner than a box cake mix (which is my usual go-to for baking) and seems runny but it cooks well.

On the griddle they need to be cooked at a lower temp than normal pancakes would or they burn. I found that a medium low worked well after some experimenting. They cook very quickly.

In really small ramekins they only need 20 minutes in the oven at 350. In the slightly larger size (which was the size I saw in the dream) it was 30 minutes.

After cooking them I tried some to make sure they were fit to offer. Without honey they are ridiculously delicious. With honey on top they are too sweet for me, but that was how I saw them so that was how I made them to offer. Obviously, my preference isn't the issue for offering cakes, but I did verify that they are edible, and in fact really good. They are also nice and simple to prepare, although they take a lot of honey.

I'll be making these for offerings to the Daoine Eile on holy days from now on and I encourage other people to consider using them as well.

End Notes

1 Honestly at this point this has happened often enough I rather think it's at least partially their way of trying to encourage me towards fluency in Irish. And I will say, although I'd hope it's obvious, that this particular situation occurs because the specific Othercrowd I am connected to are Irish and it's their language. Other people's experiences may differ radically so don't rush out to learn Irish assuming that the Good Folk will speak to you that way (although feel free to learn Irish just for the beauty of it).

2 go raibh maith agaibh Caoimhin, Lora, agus Fionnuala.

3 I am using roadkill bones for this purpose. My general preference with bones is to use those that are found rather than, shall we say, otherwise acquired.

4 another obvious use is as a simple omen where anything that appears in numbers would be counted and the count compared to that line of the charm.

5 I didn't know what these were, but I was looking for smaller cake pans and stumbled across them in the grocery store and they were the closest in size to what I had seen. I should also add here that I wouldn't recommend cooking these on or in anything made of iron.

Chapter 4

Engaging with Liminal Gods and Fairy Queens

"But as it fell out on last Halloween
When the seely court was riding by
The queen lighted down on a rowan bank
Not far frae the tree where I wont to lie"
The Ballad of Alison Gross

Generally speaking, in my practice of Fairy Witchcraft my focus isn't on deities per se as I discussed in a previous chapter. When I do honour a deity at this point I would usually look to the Fairy queen I am connected to. The wider Fairy Witchcraft tradition I am involved in has two main pairs of deities. From Bealtaine to Samhain the Lady of the Greenwood and Lord of the Wildwood hold sway as the rulers of the summer - what some may choose to call the Seelie Court - and they are powerful as well during the full moon at any time of year. From Samhain to Bealtaine the Queen of the Wind and the Hunter have dominion as rulers of winter - what some might choose to call the Unseelie Court - and as well they are powerful during the dark moon throughout the year. I've also mentioned that there are other liminal fairy gods that people may connect to and discussed a few others that I am aware of, although I don't personally connect to them. This is a fluid and evolving system and one aspect of that is the way that people will engage with these liminal Gods in their own ways.

Although I began with four, I eventually met three more before shifting more fully into focusing on a particular Fairy queen. This is, above all, a living tradition not something that is static or firmly fixed and there will always, I think, be a degree of flux with it. I want to share my process here in finding new liminal Gods, so perhaps other people can better understand how these things sometimes happen.

Lord of Mischief

It was the dark moon, and I was up on social media and a friend happened to make a comment on her own page about polytheists needing to actually focus on doing and not talking (I'm paraphrasing). And this friend tosses out an offhand comment wondering if there is a goddess of such-and-such and unbidden I find myself wondering if there is a God of Shenanigans. Because there is a long running joke at this point about myself and a propensity for shenanigans (in the sense of mischief or high-spirited behavior with maybe a small dose of secret activity). And without thinking I go to my own social media page and start typing about how if there were such a deity, surely they would be a fairy god because fairies and shenanigans go together (again paraphrasing). And I joked that perhaps I should set up a shrine....and as soon as I typed it, actually as I was typing it, I had that sense of the numinous, of presence, pressing in on me, and I thought "Oh dear".

I had found, quite without meaning to or looking, my fifth liminal fairy god. I meditated on him later and was given three names for him - titles all of them, just like the other liminal Gods prefer titles. Although they so far have stuck to single titles and this one is less settled. He told me to call him the Knight of Love, and the Keeper of Passages, and the Lord of Mischief. Shenanigans seem to sum up his nature pretty well; he is a spirit of mischief and of cleverness, of high spirits and of fun, of the sort of devilment that never really results in *permanent* harm but can be quite irritating. I rather suspect he likes to hang out wherever the fun is mighty and may in fact influence the mood and spirit of a group or place. He inspires reckless love and passion, but all in the sense of genuine enjoyment and bliss. He loves a new adventure and seeing what's around the next turn but he also guards the pathways and roads Between - because he knows them all. He loves a good joke and admires the sort of trouble that a person gets into when they are having too much fun to care. In that sense he is a rather dangerous sort, but then he's of Fairy, so that's to be expected. Safe isn't exactly something you're going to find in abundance among Themselves. I do get the sense though that as much as he may encourage you to get into trouble, he'll be equally quick to help you find your find your way out again.

I saw him as a young man, fair haired and light eyed[1]. I also got the impression of both endless sky and deep earthen tunnels around him, so again, pretty transitional. I believe his animals are foxes, otters, crows and swans. Both the colors red and white came through strongly with him, but he appeared dressed in black and green. I gather he'd like offerings of the traditional sort, milk, cream, bread, but also beer or hard liquor, and anything associated with happiness or good memories, or that symbolizes mischief by nature. He moves easily and freely between any and all times and places. I might choose to honor him especially on Samhain, as the year turns, and since I 'found' him, or he revealed himself, on the eve of the Dark moon I'd associate him with that as well.

I would also hazard to say that if it were possible for Fairy to have a trickster deity, he would be it.

Thallea and Thessilae

Unlike the others who kind of organically came to me over time and exploration, these two I found because I was specifically looking for a deity of healing that felt like they fit in with the beings I already acknowledged. It was a slow process finding the right fit here and when I did finally meet the power I was seeking I was genuinely surprised to realize it was not one but two.

They are sisters, although what they do is very different, but as I have got to know them better, I have come to believe they are like two sides of one coin despite their differences. They seem to act together as a pair and although I am not sure they are twins, per se, they seem very closely linked to each other; I have never seen them apart even when I am only trying to connect to one or the other.

Thallea[2], Lady of Roses: a power of healing and growth. I see her with skin like fresh turned earth, her hair a subtle dark green that always seems to be moving slightly, her eyes are black. Although she is focused on healing her mannerism is abrupt and brisk and I found her often impatient even though she is very kind. She is always in motion, like her hair, and rarely rests or sits still. She sings or hums when she heals and her presence is very warm. She is everything passionate about life and the struggle to live and keep living. Roses, especially pink roses, seem to be her symbol.

Thessilae[3], Lady of Thorns: a power of battle and death. I see her with skin like bone, dark hair and with black eyes like her sister. Her demeanor is calm and precise and she is a study in contrasts - still and peaceful when she is passive and a flurry of precise motion and deadly aim when she is active. I found her temperament to be much calmer and more soothing than her sister's. She may not seem at first like a healer but she is the aspect of healing that comes in the final release from suffering and pain and the transition out of the physical form. Her symbol is the blooded thorn.

An important thing to understand about these two is that in many ways they act together and they don't seem, in my experience, to differentiate at all between health and death as success in healing - both are the cessation of illness after all. They are compassionate and caring but they are, ultimately, Fey and they don't see things the same way we do; to them the spirit goes on in one form or another either with renewed physical health or freed from one body to be reborn in the next. It's just something to keep in mind if you decide to connect to them yourself.

The Seven Queens

Another evolving aspect of the wider subject is the way that the royalty of Fairy also fit in to this paradigm. In the following section we'll be discussing my theories around the connection between the Gentry and star worship in a modern context and one aspect of that is the particular importance of certain Fairy Queens. Just as we see certain pairings of Fairy Kings and Queens in folklore and practice, I have also seen seven particular Fairy Queens showing up in a group and these seven seem especially important, both in themselves and in the things that are happening in the human world today.

The Fairy Queens are strongly tied to the human world and humans, especially witches. They appear throughout folklore and recorded personal accounts directly interacting with humans, sometimes quite intimately, both for good and ill. They may be teachers imparting wisdom or skills to humans they take an interest in, or who earn their favour in some way. They may also help a human for no discernable reason, as we see in the ballad of Alison Gross. Their wider motives are unknown and largely inexplicable but the pattern of behavior is consistent across centuries and cultures.

As with most of my interactions with these sorts of beings, I prefer to use titles for them: Queen of the Greenwood, Queen of the Wind, Queen of the Wave, Queen of Stone, Queen of Flame, Queen of Horns, and the Crane Queen. Each of them is an important Fairy Queen in older folklore but is also very active in the world today as well, in her own way. Each has her own distinct personality and preferences and can be generous or dangerous depending on how one deals with her and her mood.

The Queen of the Greenwood is associated with summer and with growing things, she is slow to anger and blesses as she pleases.

The Queen of the Wind is the ruler of Winter, she teaches those she favours, punishes those who offend her, and rides the storm winds.

The Queen of the Wave is a lover of poets and has dominion over the shoreline.

The Queen of Stone heals and harms in equal measure.

The Queen of Flame is fertility, abundance, and righteous vengeance.

The Queen of Horns is beautiful or hideous as she chooses, and admires courage above all else.

The Crane Queen is both maiden and bird, both free and bound, and has special knowledge of the deep secrets of magic.

Fairy Queens in folklore and anecdotal accounts are known for their habit of showing an interest in humans in a variety of ways, and this is equally true of these seven.

End Notes

1   I'd be surprised if that has any permanence to it. I gather he can appear however he chooses, which is no surprise.

2   Thallea - Thah-lee-ah with the 'th' like in this.

3   Thessilae - Thehs-sih-lay-eh.

Chapter 5

The Pleiades, the Equinoxes, and the Fairies

"O they rade on, and farther on,
And they waded thro rivers aboon the knee,
And they saw neither sun nor moon,
But they heard the roaring of the sea."
Tam Lin, traditional ballad

Usually when I write, even when I am including personal gnosis (UPG) or personal practice, I also include a lot of references and citations to back up what I am saying. This chapter is going to be a bit different because while it will include references and citations it is something that is woven largely from personal theories and possibilities rather than provable certainties. The reader is invited to consider what is presented and take or leave it as it suits them.

I have come to a personal realization that there is a strong connection between the Good Folk and the stars, especially the Pleiades. This has been a strong factor in shaping my approach to celebrating holy days since 2018. But first some history of the Pleiades, since so much of what follows hinges on these stars and their importance across history.

The Pleiades are found across world folklore often although not always given a female nature and described as seven sisters, a mother and six daughters, or seven women (Sparavigna, 2008; White, 2016). In many of these stories the stars are numbered at seven, although occasionally they are viewed as six with a missing or hidden seventh star which may reflect the ease or difficulty of counting the stars in the constellation. In modern terms the number is much higher and, in some folklore, it can be higher as well but we will be focusing on the number seven which does seem to be the most common across mythology. The constellation is often referred to in Western culture simply as *'the Seven Sisters'* the name coming from Greek mythology which identifies each star with one of seven divine sisters. In Egypt the Pleiades where called the *'Seven Hathors'* and were represented by seven cows and a divine bull [the star Aldebaran] which provided food for the dead (Sparavigna, 2008).

The cycle of the Pleiades has changed over the millennia with their crucial rising points and significant dates shifting slowly later through the year, which must be kept in mind as we proceed. This is due to something called constellation drift, where the constellations slowly shift the times they appear in the skies over the earth across long periods. We are looking not only at when things occur now but also discussing the dating of events across thousands of years and this can be a bit confusing. That said, the Pleiades have four major processional points worth noting: when they disappear from the sky (conjunct with the sun), when they are at the eastern horizon just before dawn (heliacal rising), when they are on the eastern horizon just after sunset (acronychal rising), and when they appear directly overhead at midnight (culmination). There are also heliacal setting and acronychal setting points but I have been unable to find out anything about those dates yet. Four thousand years ago the Pleiades were conjunct with the sun at the spring equinox; the heliacal rising would occur roughly six weeks later near Bealtaine; the acronychal rising in early August; the culmination around the autumn equinox (Maunder, 1906; Sparavigna, 2008). In 2019 the conjunction occurred on May 14th, the Heliacal rising around June 23rd, the acronychal rising around September 23rd and the culmination on November 21st. The month of November is now sometimes called the month of the Pleiades (Maclure, 2017).

The Pleiades have a long and varied history around the world as timekeepers. Across many cultures the historic heliacal rising of the Pleiades marked the new year and the beginning of the spring planting season; in others these events were marked earlier in the year by the period when the Pleiades were conjunct with the sun and invisible in the sky (Maunder, 1906; Sparavigna, 2008; White, 2016). For some Native American tribes, the conjunction period was the signal to begin spring planting while in Greece the heliacal rising began the sailing season (Maclure, 2017). This would mean that thousands of years ago the spring equinox was the beginning of the new year, marked by the conjunction of the sun with the Pleiades, proceeding into the heliacal rising period about six weeks later. In contrast it has been suggested that the acronychal rising period in the autumn through the culmination in later autumn/early winter was a time when the gates to the Otherworld or spirit world where opened perhaps giving us the root of the celebration of Samhain (Maclure, 2017). In Hawaii the culmination of the Pleiades was celebrated and seen to mark the beginning of the new year (Kamehamema, 2014).

There was a time, or I should say there have been times, in Europe where the Pleiades processions, equinoxes, and fire festivals lined up exactly but that timing is fluid. As Maclure explains:

"In the 11th century, the Julian calendar used back then was about one week out of step with the seasons. In the year 1000, the September solstice fell on September 17 and the December solstice fell on December 15. Amazingly, October 31, 1000, fell about midway between these equinox and solstice dates...Some 1,000 years ago, the midnight culmination of the Pleiades and [Samhain] pretty much happened on the same date." (Maclure, 2007).

Because of equinox drift and the calendar change these events with the Pleiades now occur about 21 days later than they did a thousand years ago, meaning that for example the culmination of the Pleiades occurs on November 21st now. The conjunction with the sun occurs in May and the heliacal rising in June. Gordon White suggests that the celebration of the different Pleiadean dates was so important in India that the holidays would be shifted across quarter days as the stars slowly moved into new periods (White, 2016). This shifting system would be the one that we would have to perforce adopt as well, following the stars as they move across the seasons.

There is evidence that the Pleiades were important not only in folklore and timing major activities but also potentially for ritual activity although we can only guess. These guesses are based on alignments or depictions of the constellation at major locations that did seem to have ritual purposes. An artifact now called the 'Nebra Sky Disk' was recovered in Germany, dating from 1600 BCE and depicting the Pleiades; its purpose is unknown. Looking further back we find an array of Neolithic sites that have alignments to the equinoxes which may include the Pleiades. It is somewhat hard to be certain with some of these as archeoastronomy tends to focus heavily on solar and sometimes lunar alignments but nonetheless there is evidence of connections. In Ireland there is evidence of a Pleiadean alignment in the Gabhra valley (Halpin, 2018). Several other sites in Ireland also have alignments worth noting here. Dowth has several potential reconstructed alignments including one with Samhain that might in my opinion have been significant for the culmination of the Pleiades. Dowth more generally has potential connections to the Pleiades through its famous seven sun stone, a Neolithic stone carved with seven symbols often interpreted as suns but which may in fact represent the seven stars of the Pleiades (Murphy, 2017). Although only supposition the possibility of the symbols tying into the Pleiades also connects wider folklore about the stars to the naming-tale of Dowth which includes a story of seven cows and a bull, their owner who tried to build a tower into the sky, and his sister who held the sun still (Murphy, 2017). If we look to Sliabh na Caillagh and cairn

T we find an equinox alignment that may have included the conjunction with the Pleiades, as well as intricate engravings of suns and stars within the cairn's chamber. In Donegal Ireland we find the Grianan of Aileach which has equinox alignments and quite interestingly during the period when the rising sunlight casts a beam of light across the fort on the equinox the light points directly at the Seven Sisters mountains in the Derryveagh mountain range (Resnick, 2016). In 10,000 BCE in Turkey at Gobekli Tepe the spring equinox would have been noted by the alignment of the monument and included the Pleiades and Orion (White, 2016). The Rig Veda, drawing on astrological references dating to the same time period, talks about the importance of the Pleiades and their rising on the winter solstice (White, 2016). There is even some evidence suggesting that the Pleiades may have been noted in cave art during the paleolithic period, particularly in the cave paintings at Lascaux and La-Tête-du-Lion (Sparavigna, 2008). All of this evidence, while sometimes theoretical, nonetheless establishes the importance of these stars and hints of stellar worship which may have been obscured by later focus on solar and lunar systems.

There are also hints in the folklore and anecdotal accounts of a connection between fairies and the stars, although I admit these are only hints. In the tale of Selena Moor a human who had been taken by the fairies tells another human that the Good Folk are star worshippers (Bottrell, 1873). In a similar vein in an anecdotal account from late 19th century Ireland one man claimed the Gentry had a celestial focus (Evans-Wentz, 1911). In the ballad of Thomas the Rhymer, although there is a later reference to utter darkness, the ballad explicitly states that travelling into Fairy there is neither sun nor moon[1]; although it's tenuous one might perhaps see that as hinting at a reason why the Good Folk focus instead on stars. It is at least food for thought.

Now we move into the realm of personal gnosis, shared gnosis, and my own practices, beginning with a bit of backstory on my own connections to things Pleiadean and the equinoxes.

For decades I have worn – and now have tattooed on my arm – a seven-pointed star as a symbol of my practice. I cannot say when I started believing this or why but I have long thought it was a symbol closely connected to the Good People. There are multiple levels of meaning to this symbol but one which I have mentioned in some of my previous writing - which again I cannot remember where I first came across the idea - is that each point represents one of seven permanent or fixed gateways between the mortal world and the Otherworld. What I do know is that for several decades I have seen this symbol called a 'Pleiadean star' although I never understood the connection. Recently as I began studying this and trying to work in new personal gnosis, I think I have begun to understand the connection between the symbol, gateways, and the Pleiades. I believe for myself that this star represents the Pleiades but also the seven primary Fairy Queens and seven connections between our world and the Otherworld.

I have never put much emphasis on celebrating the equinoxes until 2017 when I had a visionary experience that included entering into an agreement with Themselves that I would make specific offerings to them on those dates. These offerings, as it was explained to me, were to open the road and keep the way open. I didn't know why those dates, but I didn't question it either as it was (at the time) a personal gnosis that didn't impact anyone else. It did oddly coincide with a belief I had long held that the Good People moved their homes at these times, something that isn't found in folklore which emphasizes Samhain and Bealtaine for those activities. Since my own work primarily focuses on connecting to the Good People, I could see the logic, I thought, in creating this sort of gateway although I had generally advised people against setting up fey highways due to the risks.

Now in September of 2018 I went to Iceland with a group and while there several of us had some interesting experiences involving the acronychal rising of the Pleiades, the autumnal equinox, and the Huldufolk. These experiences led two of us to begin theorizing that this time – the equinox and the rising of the Pleiades – was an extremely important one and a period of celebration of some sort for Themselves. It makes sense to me on an intuitive level that the Good Folk would time their holy days by the stars and not the sun or moon, which folklore and ballads tell us are lacking in Fairy. This insight into the Otherworld led to further investigation about the Pleiades more generally and resulted in some further personal gnosis via dreams. Through this I realized that the time period from the acronychal rising until culmination was a particularly important one, which they referred to [in a dream] as an 'open door'. Although I haven't received any specific guidance relating to the spring equinox and later heliacal risings, I believe the conjunction represents a still point, a 'closed door' if you will that re-opens with the heliacal rising. Perhaps not literally, any more than human holy days are literal, but energetically and ritually. These are times that I believe are sacred to the Other and I have come to believe very strongly can be - and probably historically were – sacred to humans. Perhaps they are the ones who taught us to watch those stars and celebrate those times 10,000 years ago.

Where does that leave us? Well, for myself I think I have my own folklore of the Pleiades now, still as seven sisters but as Fairy Queens. My own holidays will be changing to adapt to this new system (old system?) because I feel that it is profoundly important. I haven't worked out all the details yet, specifically when it makes sense to honor the new year[2], but I know that these four main points are times to celebrate and I can work with that. The acronychal rising is the Opening of the Door. The culmination is the Celestial Fairy Rade. The conjunction is the Darkening. The heliacal rising is the Return of the Queens. The equinoxes are times to offer to them, specifically focused on opening the roads, while the other two holy days are more purely celebratory in nature, honoring the connection that has been created and reaffirming it. Because these dates by nature slowly move through the year none of these holidays focus on or emphasize specific earthly events or times, such as planting or harvesting but are designed to be flexible and fit wherever they fall.

I won't deny that I'm feeling entirely untethered at the idea of moving forward and away from a luni-solar holiday cycle that I have used for decades. I think it's going to take a few years of experimentation, at least, to get this new system fine-tuned and worked out and part of why I am writing about this is because I would like to make this a co-creative project. I'd welcome anyone else who feels drawn to (or even just curious about) this sort of holiday cycle. Obviously, this entire system will be as much my own intuition and gnosis as research and facts, but I hope it will have value for people beyond myself.

I have been doing as much research as possible on the Pleiades themselves and their various worldwide folklore and I have also been trying to connect to my own spiritual gnosis on the topic. I wrote at the start of this chapter some of my basic findings about the Pleiades, but please understand that is barely touching the breadth of material out there. The Pleiades and their importance are a worldwide phenomenon and they can be found to some degree in all cultures I have looked at. It is simply too much to cover all of it here.

I have spent a year working out a modern schedule based on the Pleiadean cycle. I had already uncovered four: the conjunction with the sun which occurs around old Bealtaine (mid-May), the heliacal rising six weeks later in June (theoretically around the solstice), the acronychal rising (around the autumnal equinox), and the culmination (Nov. 21). I feel like there are at least two more significant Pleiadean dates, but so far, I am unsure when those may be, if they even exist. I'm still working on this and of course actually following the stars for a year or several will help flesh out the structure. I'll probably add in a seventh holiday just because I like the number, possibly the winter solstice. I think that the spring equinox is also an important time, if only because the Pleiades used to align there for the conjunction and that was a very sacred time across many cultures but again at this point, I am unsure how it will fit itself in. Moving from a luni-solar ritual cycle into a stellar one has been a huge shift for me.

The cycle as I've been able to piece it together so far is based on the four key points I have mentioned previously. I have names for these points in line with my own spirituality and am slowly intuiting stories connected to them. Obviously, this is only the very beginning of sorting out this cycle and more importantly of figuring out the key ritual points to acknowledge, but it is a beginning.

My personal preference right now is to tentatively call these dates:

The conjunction, May 14th: The Darkening
The heliacal rising, June 23rd: The Return of the Queens (or just the Returning)
The acronychal rising, September 23rd: The Way-Opening
The culmination, November 21st: The Celestial Fairy Rade

I have some tentative story around these, I wouldn't call it mythology, of course, because it's new, but stories seems accurate. I think it's important though that these not just be new dates for the holidays we already have, exactly, but rather that we acknowledge these are both old and new. Yes, I do believe that the Pleiades were celebrated as the original markers for certain holy days - and world mythology supports this of course - but because of the drift in timing we can't just go back to that. The conjunction isn't in late March anymore it's in May; the heliacal rising isn't in May it's in June. That makes a significant difference when these aren't just static dates but also living traditions. The mythology and focuses that we do have for the oldest stories of the Pleiades don't work anymore when the timing has shifted so radically. We have to find the threads of the old and the hints of the significance this may have had for us in our own forms of historic paganism, and even back before into the roots of the Neolithic and bronze ages, and then work those traces into a viable modern system.

When I see the Pleiades, it looks to me like a blue bonfire burning in the sky and I can imagine it easily as a gathering place of celestial Queens, of Fairy Queens, of seven Divine Sisters. When the star-fire that is the Pleiades disappears from the night sky the Queens have parted ways and left their Courts. Maybe they are travelling on earth. Maybe they are searching for something. Maybe they are sowing change or strife or beginnings or endings. They each have their own agendas. When the constellation returns to the horizon the Queens have returned, gathered together again to exchange news and share stories. When the stars rise at sunset it represents the Opening of the Way Between Worlds, when the dead and Good Folk and Others have more freedom to move within our world. The culmination is when the Fairy Rades ride out, and the Wild Hunt is especially active.

I suspect that the time in late December and early January as well as around the spring equinox are also very important but I haven't quite gotten the pieces together yet for those. My gut tells me that the December/January period represents a point of high activity for the Otherworld and so perhaps another key Pleiadean date and that the spring equinox may connect to the new year.

As to the Queens? There is a lot of lore around the Pleiades that a person can easily use and much of it relates the seven stars to women. For myself I have come to see them as seven Fairy Queens because that is what makes sense to me. I discussed them a bit in the previous chapter and I hope this section has shown the ways that I see them tying into the Pleiades, although

I admit I don't fully understand the depth of it myself. For me though the seven main stars represent the Queens in the sky, with Aldebaran as the Hunter, a Fairy King who follows them and guards their journey. The cycle of the Pleaides through the year is the cycle of these Queens, symbolizing their waning and waxing presence in the human world, their holding court in the sky, their ride with their gathered people. Each holy day is a time to remember and acknowledge the Queens and this eternal journey and to remember the intrinsic joining of the two worlds, Fairy and earth.

End Notes

1   In fairness it is also possible that this is a reference to a time such as the dark moon when the sky would be without either sun or moon at night.

2   The spring equinox was viewed as the date of the new year until the 18th century in the United States and parts of Europe, and I'm really chewing on that right now. However it is also significant to me that in Hawaii it was is the culmination in November that is understood to be the new year and this could also be a viable https://www.bostonglobe.com/ideas/2014/03/22/march-happy-colonial-new-year/L0MrkQc47SiUu1OHVJt1lI/story.html

Chapter 6

Rituals for the Pleiades

"The morn is Halloweven night,
the elfin court will ride,
Through England, and thro a' Scotland,
And through the world wide."
Tam Lin, traditional ballad

In this chapter I will share the cycle of four rituals I have designed and used over the last year. Each ritual section ends with my own personal notes about my experiences with that ritual and the chapter ends with my overall notes for the entire cycle. I want to include my notes so that anyone following along with this can see my process in both creating these rituals and also recording my own progress through the first year. This is only the beginning of what I think will be a lifelong journey for me so I suspect this will all grow and become more detailed as time goes by.

Ritual to Honour the Culmination of the Pleiades
The first holy day in my new cycle is the culmination of the Pleiades which occurs at midnight on 21 November.

My own approach to ritual tends to be a bit more casual than some other people's so what follows shouldn't be viewed as rigidly structured but as flexible and adaptable to your own personal style. The only things that are absolutely required (besides good manners) are extending the invitation to the Other, making an appropriate offering, and celebrating Their presence.

The offering that I will be referring to and making in this ritual is one that I use when I am home and able to cook. It is a recipe that came to me in a dream once and which I have written about before, for small honey cakes that I call Cáca Síofra.

The Celestial Fairy Rade

We are in the season when the gates to Fairy are open wide and stories abound of encounters between unwitting mortals and processions - or rades[1] - of the Good People as well as more dangerous encounters with the Wild Hunt. From the end of September until roughly the end of January, or put another way from the fall equinox until the old end of Yule[2], the Fair Folk were known to be more active and potentially more dangerous. More active is of course a matter of degrees and perspective. The month of November is sometimes known as the month of the Pleiades because it is during this month that the constellation is visible during the entire night and on 21 November the Pleiades culminate, appearing at the height of the sky at exactly midnight. This occurs in the middle of this high point in Otherworldly activity.

I have come to believe that this culmination is a very important time for the Otherworld and that those of us who feel very in tune with the Other can choose to celebrate this time as well. These holy days are celebrations of the Otherworld's connection to ours rather than the common holiday focus in paganism on agricultural or seasonal events.

Ritual

Find a good space open beneath the sky where you can see the stars above you. If this is not possible due to weather concerns try to set up an altar near a window or perhaps arrange some appropriate artwork near your ritual space. If necessary, this entire thing can be done as a visualization exercise. My own outdoor altar for ritual work usually contains space for offerings, water in an appropriate container, candles, and a token representing the Fairy Queen I honour.

Create sacred space as you see fit if you wish to. I usually do this now by moving counterclockwise around my space sprinkling water and chanting to open the way between worlds.

Invite in any Powers you wish to. This is not a ritual for named Gods unless they are explicitly associated with the Good People of one culture or another. This is a time to invite any goodly inclined spirits, allies, Fairy Queens or Kings, or Liminal Gods in. We invite, we don't invoke, evoke, or compel. They either come as we call or they don't. I might say something like:

"I call to all goodly inclined spirits,
spirits of the land, spirits of the air,
Fair Folk who would be my friends,
Friendly ones who aid my liminal path,
Liminal gods, Fairy Queens and Kings,
My wonderous Lady ---,
Queen of stone and well,
I invite you all to join me here
As I honour the journey
Of the celestial Fairy Rade"

After this is done wait a moment and observe. Use all your sense to note if there is any obvious response to your call. This may be obvious, such as the wind picking up or the temperature changing, or it may be a more subtle feeling of presence. don't rush but wait until things feel settled. Say:

"Tonight the Seven Queens are at their height
standing in the center of the sky
in the middle point of night
Their fair blue light burns brightly
A beacon in the darkness
The Fairy Rade rides
Forth between worlds
The gates are open, may

They be opened wider
The Queens look upon the land
May they bless what they see"
Put out the offerings you have brought and pour out a bit of
water.
"I offer sweet honey cakes [or whatever you are offering]
And pure clean water
To the queens
To the liminal gods
To those beings that
would aid me
to the spirits of air
and of earth"

At this point if there is anything else you would like to do in
your ritual - sing, dance, chant, divination, meditate, journey -
do it. When you feel ready to say goodbye, say:

"The Queens light up the sky
The Fairy Rades ride across the land
Our worlds are intertwined
As they have been and will be
Praise to the Queens,
May they bless us
A good word to the Fairy Rade
May they cause us no harm"
Pour out the water that is left. Say
"May my words honour the Queens
May my actions honour the liminal Gods
May my allies stand with me
May there be peace between me
And the spirits of the air and earth
May there be friendship between me
And all goodly inclined spirits."

Take down your compass/circle or sacred space however you normally would. In my case here I'd walk it clockwise sprinkling a bit of earth or leaves and asking that the space be returned to its former state. Take down your altar.

Ritual Feast

Part of my own celebration will include a feast or ritual meal the following day. This is in line with some older practices that would see the night before as the beginning of the ritual date and the following day as its continuation and would incorporate ritual feasting into the process. My plan is to do the ritual itself at midnight but treat the following day as a holiday, with small gifts for my family and a big meal the next evening. A portion of that meal will be set aside and then left out as an additional offering. I will also look at taking omens the next morning.

My Personal Experience

This is an account of my first time celebrating this ritual.

Going out under the November sky last night in the US was strongly reminiscent of being out at night in Iceland for me. It was unusually cold and windy, the air having that sharpness that it gets when the temperature is a good amount below freezing.

I had intended to make offerings of honey cakes which I have used before on major holidays but there was an odd amount of apple synchronicity going on during the day so after some divination work I ended up making an apple spice cake instead. There seemed to be a very strong apple theme all around which is something I will certainly keep in mind next year. As it was, I moved out into the darkness of the late night carrying fresh water and apple cake to offer, searching the sky for the blue glow of the Pleiades. Since the full moon was also high in the sky, I had some trouble finding the stars but I did eventually locate them and I set up in what I felt was a good spot.

I cast my compass using some of the water, not for protection but asking that the way between worlds be opened. I spoke the beginning portion of the ritual, inviting in the Otherworldly powers, and froze as the sound of bells and uncanny music floated on the wind. It was unnerving; the last time I'd heard anything like that when the Slua Sidhe was nearby and I can't quite put into words the way it makes you feel terrified and thrilled all at once. I stood my ground and went on to the next part trying to ignore the sound of shuffling footsteps in the leaves around me. After that section I did pause again to make sure there weren't any animals nearby as I wasn't eager to be surprised by - or surprise - any local wildlife. Suffice to say that it wasn't wildlife making the noises so I continued on with the rest of it.

At the very end as I was closing up there was a particularly large gust of wind then everything went very still. It felt good in that moment, the whole ritual felt good if a bit wild and certainly eldritch in the old sense.

Someone inside the house would tell me later that while I was outside our entire house shook in a way that made them think a branch had fallen on the roof although there was no accompanying noise with it and no damage or sign of anything amiss today. I had strange dreams last night and today has been an interesting day overall but again nothing bad just a bit more intensely Otherworldly than usual.

We are finishing out our new holiday celebration with a feast incorporating apples in as many ways as I can manage. Some of this will also be left out as an offering of course. I feel that this was successful and intend to celebrate it again next year.

Notes

I think the apple theme is important and as I look at celebrating this again, I want to make that more of a focal point. I can carry it through as a theme of the holy day intentionally rather than have it happen by accident.

Overall, I think the ritual went really well and the structure around it seems sound. I will continue using this structure going forward.

End Notes

1   Rade is a Scots word that means ride but is associated with ceremonial processions.

2   Based on the dates before the calendar changes which would place the end of the yule season about 11 days later than it is now, if we are timing it by calendar dates.

The Conjunction of the Pleiades: The Darkening

The next ritual in the cycle is the conjunction with the sun which occurs around old Bealtaine (mid-May) - this year on May 14th. I'd recommend doing this ritual during the day, when the sun is up as this is also when the Pleiades are in the sky now.

The Darkening

As I mentioned in the previous chapter this holiday is the time when the Pleiades disappear from the sky for the next six weeks. I have been calling it the Darkening. My own personal mythology around this event is about the Queens travelling out. When the star-fire that is the Pleiades disappears from the night sky the Queens have parted ways and left their individual Courts. Each Queen has her own motivations and reasons for travelling and we can only guess at what these may be. This time would mark a slight still point in the energetic year but also a time when contact with the Queens and their denizens increases as it does between the Achronycal Rising and Culmination. Unlike the autumn season the Darkening is gentler time, comparatively.

I have tried to keep this ritual fairly similar in outline and flow to the other one, to help with the continuity. I will use a similar format in all of the rituals for this series.

Ritual

Find a good space open beneath the sky where you can see the sun above you. If this is not possible due to weather concerns try to set up an altar near a window or perhaps arrange some appropriate artwork near your ritual space. If necessary, this entire thing can be done as a visualization exercise. My own outdoor altar for ritual work usually contains space for offerings, water in an appropriate container, candles, and a token representing the Fairy Queen I honour.

Bring some food to offer, perhaps honey cakes, and clean water to pour out. Create sacred space as you see fit if you wish to. I have found my method of walking counterclockwise sprinkling water and chanting to open the way between worlds quite effective. Invite in any Powers you wish to. This is a time to invite any goodly inclined spirits, allies, Fairy Queens or Kings in. I might say something like:

"I call to all goodly inclined spirits,
spirits of the land, spirits of the air,
Fair Folk who would be my friends,
Friendly ones who aid my liminal path,
Fairy Queens and Kings,
My wonderous Lady ---,
Queen of stone and well,
I invite you all to join me here
As I honour the journey
Of the celestial Fairy Rade"

You can tailor this initiation as suits you and whatever Queen or Spirit you are calling.

After this is done wait a moment and observe. Use all your senses to note if there is any perceptible response to your call. This may be obvious, such as the wind picking up or the temperature changing, or it may be a more subtle feeling of presence. Don't rush but wait until things feel settled before moving on. Say:

"Today the Seven Queens leave the sky
Leaving darkness for day
Separating to their own paths
Their powers burn as brightly
Whether they stand together or apart
But our world is fuller for their presence

They ride out for good and ill
Between worlds, between time
The gates are open, may
They be opened wider
The Queens look upon the land
May they bless what they see[1]"

Put out the offerings you have brought and pour out a bit of water.

"I offer sweet honey cakes [or whatever you are offering]
And pure, clean water
To the Queens
To the Good Neighbours
To those beings that
would aid me
to the spirits of air
and of earth"

At this point if there is anything else you would like to do in your ritual - sing, dance, chant, divination, meditate, journey - do it. When you feel ready to say goodbye, say:

"The seven stars have left the sky
The Queens ride across the land
Our worlds are intertwined
As they have been and will be
Praise to the Queens,
May they bless us
A good word to the Fair Folk
May they cause us no harm"

Pour out the water that is left. Say:

"May my words praise the Queens
May my actions show respect to the Good Folk
May my allies stand with me
May there be peace between me
And the spirits of the air and earth
May there be friendship between me
And all goodly inclined spirits."

Take down your compass/circle or sacred space however you normally would. In my case here I'd walk it clockwise sprinkling a bit of earth or leaves and asking that the space be returned to its former state. Take down your altar. Leave the offerings out. Perhaps take a moment to stop and listen, look, feel the energy around you. See if there is anything worth noting or any sense of presence.

Ritual Feast

Part of my own celebration will include a feast or ritual meal. This is in line with some older practices that would incorporate ritual feasting into the celebration of holy days. My plan is to have a special meal featuring fresh vegetables and fruits, fish, and ideally anything that could be wild gathered this early (obviously that would vary greatly by region). A portion of that meal will be set aside and then left out as an additional offering. I will also take omens about 12 hours after the ritual to get a feel for how things went, the wider energy, and the next six weeks.

If the theories behind these rituals hold true then the time between the conjunction and the heliacal rising should be intense energetically and represent a time of changes, good or bad, of endings and beginnings, and of increased Otherworldly activity.

My Personal Experience

I did my ritual for the conjunction of the Pleiades yesterday, about midday. It was interesting.

The ritual in November for the culmination was intense, the wind died down, everything got very quiet, I could sense and hear unseen things shuffling around nearby. This one was also intense but in rather the opposite way. Once it began everything seemed to ramp up. Squirrels appeared and were hopping around nearby, the bird song got noticeably louder, and an owl started calling (only during the ritual). Honestly not what I was expecting and a bit distracting.

Overall it had a good feel to it though so I'm pretty satisfied.

Notes

Based on the suggestion to include a welcoming of the Queens I am going to amend the main section of the ritual to this (I'll put the new section in italics):

"Today the Seven Queens leave the sky
Leaving darkness for day
Separating to their own paths
Their powers burn as brightly
Whether they stand together or apart
But our world is fuller for their presence
They ride out for good and ill
Between worlds, between time
We welcome them back to mortal earth
Looking for their presence
And seeking their blessings
In our lives and our world
We welcome them back
The gates are open, may
They be opened wider
The Queens look upon the land
May they bless what they see."

If you choose to do this ritual you may use either version.

End Note

1   My friend Steve did suggest adding something about welcoming the Queens back to the land so I may tweak that for next time, because it's a good idea. Not just to acknowledge their presence but actively welcome them.

Ritual for the Heliacal Rising of the Pleiades

Continuing with our series of rituals for the cycle of the Pleiades we have arrived at the next one, the heliacal rising of the Pleiades after their conjunction with the sun. This marks the time when the stars are once again visible in the sky just before dawn and occurs now between June 18th and June 24th. You can choose to do it early in the day, close to when the Pleiades are in the sky now; you may also choose to celebrate the night before, perhaps including some midsummer traditions like a bonfire into your celebration. My own preference is to celebrate on the 23rd into the 24th, the liminal time just on the edge of both the end of the Pleiades rising and also the end of the solstice alignment. There is also a great deal of fairy folklore connected to that date which I enjoy incorporating as well.

This holiday acknowledges the return of the Pleiades to the sky after a six weeks absence. I have been calling it the Return of the Queens, or the Returning. My own personal mythology around this event ties it strongly to the previous holiday where the Queens travelled out into our world, symbolized by the loss of the stars from the night sky. Now we see them returning from their travels, leaving our world to return to their own. When the star-fire that is the Pleiades returns to the night sky the Queens have returned to their celestial Courts, figuratively speaking. This ritual also acknowledges another sacred star, Aldebaran, part of the constellation of Taurus which has been tied to the mythology of the Pleiades in many cultures. Aldebaran appears to follow the Pleiades through the sky - hence the meaning of the name in Arabic[1] - but I call it the Hunter, after one of the liminal Gods in fairy witchcraft. In this case of course he isn't hunting the seven Queens but protecting them as they travel across the sky.

Ritual

Find a good space open beneath the sky. If this is not possible due to weather concerns try to set up an altar near a window or perhaps arrange some appropriate artwork near your ritual space. However, if necessary, this entire thing can be done as a visualization exercise. My own outdoor altar for ritual work usually contains space for offerings, water in an appropriate container, candles, and a token representing the Fairy Queen I honour.

Bring some food to offer, perhaps honey cakes, and clean water to pour out.

Create sacred space as you see fit if you wish to. There is no right or wrong here as long as you aren't warding out the same spirits you are trying to invite in, so go with whatever you feel most connected to as a method.

Invite in any Powers you wish to but remember this is not a ritual for named Gods unless they are explicitly associated with the Good People of one culture or another. This is a time to invite any goodly inclined spirits, allies, Fairy Queens or Kings in. I might say something like:

"I call to all goodly inclined spirits,
spirits of the land, spirits of the air,
Fair Folk who would be my friends,
Friendly ones who aid my liminal path,
Fairy Queens and Kings,
My wonderous Lady ---,
Queen of stone and well,
I invite you all to join me here
As I honour the journey
Of the Queens and
the Return of the stars"

You can tailor this initiation as suits you and whatever Queen or Spirit you are calling. After this is done wait a moment and observe. Use all your senses to note if there is any perceptible response to your call. This may be obvious, such as the wind picking up or the temperature changing, or it may be a more subtle feeling of presence. Don't rush but wait until things feel settled before moving on. Say:

"Today the Seven Queens return to the sky
Moving from daylight to darkness
Rejoining the stars, proceeding
The great guarding light of the Hunter*
Their bright blue fire a blazing torch
a beacon in the predawn night sky
a new cycle begins in the growing darkness
As they tread again the celestial path
The gates are open, may
They be opened wider
The Queens look upon the land
May they bless what they see"

Put out the offerings you have brought and pour out a bit of water.

"I offer sweet honey cakes [or whatever you are offering]
And pure, clean water
To the Queens
To the Good Neighbours
To those beings that
would aid me
to the spirits of air
and of earth"

At this point if there is anything else you would like to do in your ritual - sing, dance, chant, divination, meditate, journey -

do it. When you feel ready to say goodbye, say:

> *"The Seven Queens return to the sky*
> *The Queens have travelled our world*
> *And return again to their own*
> *Standing in the space between*
> *Our worlds are intertwined*
> *As they have been and will be*
> *Praise to the Queens,*
> *May they bless us*
> *A good word to the Fair Folk*
> *May they cause us no harm"*

Pour out the water that is left. Say:

> *"May my words praise the Queens*
> *May my actions show respect to the Good Folk*
> *May my allies stand with me*
> *May there be peace between me*
> *And the spirits of the air and earth*
> *May there be friendship between me*
> *And all goodly inclined spirits."*

Take down your compass/circle or sacred space however you normally would. In my case here I'd walk it clockwise sprinkling a bit of earth or leaves and asking that the space be returned to its former state. Take down your altar. Leave the offerings out. Perhaps take a moment to stop and listen, look, feel the energy around you. See if there is anything worth noting or any sense of presence.

Ritual Feast

As with the other rituals I will include a ritual feast with this holy day. My plan is to have a special meal featuring fresh vegetables and fruits, and ideally anything that could be wild gathered or otherwise harvested this time of year (obviously that would vary greatly by region). A portion of that meal will be set aside and then left out as an additional offering. I will also take omens about 12 hours after the ritual to get a feel for how things went and the wider energy going on.

If the theories and previous experiences with these rituals hold true then the time of the heliacal rising should be one of intense energy and potential interaction with the Otherworld. Even though we are celebrating it as a time when the Queens are returning to the Courts, symbolized by the return of the Pleiades to the night sky, this isn't an instantaneous switch - just like the summer solstice marks a pivotal point where the daylight starts to wane slowly, the heliacal rising marks the point when the Pleiades begin to shift back into the night from the day but this is a process. They will not be fully in the night, from dusk until dawn, until the culmination in November.

My Personal Experience

I went out early in the morning, as close to dawn as I could manage. When I first set the space and invited the powers in, I waited and there was a noticeable lull in the wind but an increase in bird song, reminiscent of the ritual in May. I took that as a good omen. I proceeded with the body of the ritual and I felt like there was a noticeable increase in presence around me although this is hard to measure objectively. The ritual itself had a peaceful feeling to it. Overall the energy of the entire thing was noticeably stiller and more peaceful than the others.

Notes

This was the first ritual of the series where I felt like time shifted a bit, as I felt like the ritual passed quickly but when I was done it had actually been about 20 minutes.

End Note

1 Aldebaran 'the follower' also called the eye of the bull for its position in Taurus.

Ritual for the Pleiades: The Way Opening

This holy day occurs at the time of year of the acronychal rising of the Pleiades, when they are on the eastern horizon just after full dark, or roughly about 9pm for my latitude, This coincides with the general date of the autumn equinox and I personally choose to celebrate my ritual for it on the equinox. In my constructed mythology this is the time of the Opening of the Way Between Worlds, when the Good Neighbours have more freedom to move within our world, as do the human dead and other types of spirits.

The Opening of the Way is the fourth and final ritual in the cycle as it exists now, although symbolically it is the beginning of the cycle.

Opening of the Way Between Worlds

There is no point when the way between worlds is closed but there are times when the ways are wider and narrower. Something like the tide, it ebbs and flows. Also, there are places in our world that have been slowly cut off from Fairy, where that energy and influence have been pushed back by other powers. At certain times of year, the way to Fairy narrows, the energy that can be felt in this world lessens a bit; at others most notably in my own experience the heliacal and acronychal rising of the Pleiades, this energy increases in ways that humans perceive. It's a palpable shift. This ritual is designed to invite in and encourage this energy and this opening. It is also intended to invite the energy of Fairy back into the places where it has been pushed out over the last thousand years or so. Re-aligning and righting the balance. In this sense it is perhaps the most essential of the four.

Ritual

I recommend doing this ritual close to full dark, ideally when the Pleiades have risen or are visible on the horizon. Find a good space open beneath the sky where you can see the stars. If this is not possible due to weather concerns try to set up an altar near a window or perhaps arrange some appropriate artwork near your ritual space. If necessary, this entire thing can be done as a visualization exercise. My own outdoor altar for ritual work usually contains space for offerings, water in an appropriate container, candles, and a token representing the Fairy Queen I honour.

Create sacred space as you see fit if you wish to. Invite in any Powers you wish to. I might say something like:

"I call to all goodly inclined spirits,
spirits of the land, spirits of the air,
Fair Folk who would be my friends,
Friendly ones who aid my liminal path,
Liminal gods, Fairy Queens and Kings,
My wonderous Lady ---,
Queen of stone and well,
I invite you all to join me here
As I honour the Opening
Of the Way Between Worlds"

After this is done wait a moment and observe. Use all your sense to note if there is any obvious response to your call. This may be obvious, such as the wind picking up or the temperature changing, or it may be a more subtle feeling of presence. don't rush but wait until things feel settled. Say:

"Tonight the Seven Queens rise in the east,
Standing on the horizon,
as daylight falls to night

73

Their eldritch blue light burns brightly
A signal fire calling us back to them
The Queens dance at the world's edge
between worlds, between time,
The way that has been narrowed
Is now a road, fair and broad
The door that stood cracked
Is now being pushed to fullness
The gates are open, may
They be opened wider
The Queens look upon the land
May they bless what they see"

Put out the offerings you have brought and pour out a bit of water.

"I offer sweet honey cakes [or whatever you are offering]
And pure clean water
To the queens
To the liminal gods
To those beings that
would aid me
to the spirits of air
and of earth"

At this point if there is anything else you would like to do in your ritual - sing, dance, chant, divination, meditate, journey - do it. When you feel ready to say goodbye, say:

"The Queens light up the sky
The way between worlds is open
Our worlds are intertwined
As they have been and will be
Praise to the Queens,

May they bless us
A good word to the Fairy Rade
May they cause us no harm"
Pour out the water that is left. Say
"May my words honour the Queens
May my actions honour the liminal Gods
May my allies stand with me
May there be peace between me
And the spirits of the air and earth
May there be friendship between me
And all goodly inclined spirits."

Take down your compass/circle or sacred space however you normally would. In my case here I'd walk it clockwise sprinkling a bit of earth or leaves and asking that the space be returned to its former state. Take down your altar.

Ritual Feast

Part of my own celebration will include a feast or ritual meal the following day, as I have with all the others. My plan is to do the ritual itself at midnight but treat the following day as a holiday, with small gifts for my family and a big meal the next evening. This is also in keeping with the more significant nature of this particular holiday. A portion of that meal will be set aside and then left out as an additional offering. I will also look at taking omens the next morning.

My Personal Experience

I held this ritual around 9 pm I wasn't able to see the Pleiades due to weather conditions but I used a star tracker app on my phone to ascertain their location and be sure they were above the horizon. When I began the invocation portion the wind picked up slightly and I could hear an owl in the woods (not unusual this time of year although I will note that it was silent before and afterwards). The ritual itself was quiet and the energy seemed more watchful than anything else. When I was doing the final parting part the neighbourhood dogs began barking and all stopped as I finished.

Notes

This time I tried doing it without casting any circle, even the basic tuathail water casting I have been using, and there was an obviously lower level of engagement and activity. I'm not entirely sure what the connection there is but it seems clear that opening with a tuathail compass casting even in a basic form does allow for more crossover than without it. Because of this I will be using the simple water compass casting in all my rituals moving forward.

Notes After One Full Year

Overall, I feel that this ritual cycle was successful and I am both excited to continue moving forward with this and also encouraged that I am on the right track connecting the Pleiades to Holy Day rituals and the Othercrowd. It remains to be seen what the wider affects and uses of this will be and I am going to continue to study the connection between stellar alignments and fairylore. I believe this is a good, viable start however and will be continuing to build on this base.

There were several other people who also did these rituals and shared their results on social media. Everyone reported varying degrees of response or engagement with the Other, as well as increased activity for a period of time around them. I am encouraged by this feedback that these rituals are sound and will be effective for not just for me but also for other people who try them.

My goal in the coming year – cycle 2 – is to build on the mythology structured around these dates, seek further connections with them in existing folklore, and work on creating my own personal traditions and celebrations with them. These are specifically aimed at solitary or small group work and I feel they would not be adaptable to anything else. As a parent I would like to try to find ways to expand the holy days outwards to have aspects that would be applicable to families and children, and outer ring if you will, while preserving these rituals as an inner practice of active witches.

I am hopeful that this process is only a bare beginning of something much bigger.

Conclusion

There is a stream of historic witchcraft that is intrinsically tied to fairies, and arguably the Fair Folk themselves are symbiotically bound to humanity. Yet we have forgotten that over time, just as we have forgotten who the Good Folk really are and, in some case, where some witches really got their power from.

I've often said that I think witchcraft, specifically neopagan witchcraft in the US, is a victim of its own public relations. This is something we can see more and more clearly as different divides appear within the wider community, often over core issues of inclusion or exclusion. Why do these things happen in witchcraft which is at its core something that should be amorphous enough to hold a place for everyone?

Because, I think, we have forgotten where witchcraft came from, where its power is rooted.

There's been a push for decades, since the 1950's at least in my opinion, towards mainstreaming witchcraft and painting a picture of it as gentle and kind. Reimagining witchcraft as the domain of the white middle class, literally recasting the witch as young and white and female - and of course beautiful. Harmless. And intending no harm either. The exact same thing that has been done to fairies over the last hundred years and with the same results.

This idea has been pushed so hard and for so long that many of us have started to believe it ourselves, and there's a whole generation of witches now who see witchcraft as an aesthetic of young, beautiful, spooky (but harmless!) people. Looking like Morticia Addams but with candles and a cat.

Maybe there's nothing wrong with that, and I have no issue with people whose witchcraft is gentle or based on lighting candles and thinking good thoughts. Witchcraft is expansive, it can fit these new people in.

But many have lost and intentionally subsumed the other (and the Other for that matter) along the way. They have accepted a certain degree of trendy outsider but only so far, only what is still acceptable to the wider mainstream. They hate being embarrassed by those people[1], the ones who make the mainstream witches look bad by going too far, by being too queer, too ethnic, too macabre, too spirit-ridden, too dramatic, too big, too different, too outside the norm. Too much. Being in service to a Fairy Queen? Definitely too far. Making pacts with spirits? Too early modern witchcraft. Necromancy? Too Hollywood. Oh, mainstream witches may talk about all of these things repackaged into more palatable forms but the real gritty bloody practices no. And then there's the people who are politely segregated, the ones who are told to make their own spaces and get out of the rest, the people of color, the transpeople, the gender non-conforming, people from specific cultures. Actual inclusion is messy. It's intersectional and difficult and requires making space and letting people speak for themselves instead of speaking for them.

They talk a lot about spirits and fairies but we don't seem to actual live that talk. There are no teeth to the belief. Pun intended.

They have forgotten the power of feasting with the Devil and dancing with the Queen of Elphame. They have forgotten the need to heal with magic when there is no money to heal with doctors.

They have forgotten the rage of the unheard victim who knows they will find no justice in any court and turns instead to a moonless night and thorns and clay.

Because it's easy when a person lives in relative comfort and safety, when danger is an idea rather than a reality, to forget the visceral needs that drove and still drive people to feast and dance and heal and hex. It's easy to forget when a person is part of the comfortable majority, in any sense, what it's like for those who are not, who live on the fringes. For those who don't choose witchcraft for gentle reasons but for survival and defiance. The disabled, the queer, the marginalized, the unwanted. And the people for whom witchcraft isn't a choice but an inheritance, a culture, a way of life. People who learn their witchcraft from spirits. People for whom witchcraft is about power.

It's easy to embrace the fictional fairies and the ones cavorting through children's books when the fairies of folklore and the thin places, the fairies of liminal times and of random encounters, are neither safe nor gentle. When the sanitized versions are shaped by human control and centered on human importance in contrast to the folklore of fairies as sexual, and boundary crossing, and dangerous. When the fairies of anecdotes are as likely to bless as maim. When they follow their own rules, which are not ours to shape. We need to remember all of these things.

Our world – our western cultural world – is broken. It's been broken for a thousand years since the Othercrowd first started being forced out and the brokenness has finally reached a tipping point. The Other is fighting back, fighting its way back into this world. It's time we start fighting as well to bring them back fully into the world rather than leave them lurking at the edges. To return things to the way they were before, when the Other was invested here. It's time to start living in our own power, to get our hands dirty and bloody again, to go out under the stars and feast and dance. To embrace defiance. And to look to older truths about the Good Neighbours to shape our understandings as well as guide us in this restoration.

Reconnecting to this raw witchcraft is essential as you move deeper into connecting to the Fair Folk. Strip away the dross and you will find what has true value – and in that where your real power lies.

I started this by talking about re-enchanting – restoring - the world. Offering to the Good Folk on the equinoxes and following the cycle of the Pleiades are ways I think we can do that. We can open the door and re-build the old connections, even if this means a human world that is more spirit-filled and wilder. Not everything of the Otherworld is safe or gentle but we need Them as much as they need us and our world needs the balance they provide. And our witchcraft will be richer for their presence.

End Note

1   My usual disclaimer that no I do not mean actual predators or dangerous people here. They deserve to be shunned and should be.

Appendix A: Resources

I draw on a lot of resources for my own practice of witchcraft, and at this point I've moved away (for the most part) from looking at how other modern practitioners do things and instead draw on ideas about how historic witchcraft was likely done. I combine that with folk magic practices and the Fairy Faith to create the practical system that I use for my witchcraft. Here is a list of some of the main academic sources that I use:

'Cunning Folk and Familiar Spirits' and 'The Visions of Isobel Gowdie' by Emma Wilby. Two of my top sources, they deal with both early modern witchcraft as well as touching on fairy beliefs and practices.

'Popular Magic: Cunning-folk in English History' by Owen Davies. Another good look at early modern magical practices which includes some fairy beliefs.

'Between the Living and the Dead' by Eva Pócs. A look at early modern witchcraft practices in eastern Europe.

'The Witch Figure' edited by Venetia Newall. A collection of essays on witchcraft in folklore and across different cultures. Quite a bit of fascinating and useful material.

'Witches, Werewolves, and Fairies' by Claude Lecouteux. A look at the soul complex within European belief but includes a lot of valuable lore about witches and fairies that is applicable to practice. I found it especially relevant for dream work and journeying.

'Scottish Fairy Belief' by Lizanne Henderson and Edward Cowan. Primarily focused on fairy beliefs (and also on my list for that subject) but this book includes a good amount of witchcraft material as well, including some actual methods of dealing with fairies used by cunningfolk.

'Witchcraft and Magic in Ireland' by Andrew Sneddon. Not

actually one of my favorites as I find the title deceptive - its focus is more on the outbreaks of witchcraft accusations among protestant communities in Ireland. However, it does touch to some degree on folk practices and Irish witchcraft in the final chapter so it has its uses.

'The Silver Bough' by F Marian McNeill. A look at Scottish folk beliefs more generally it includes some very useful sections on witchcraft and fairy beliefs.

'Elf Queens and Holy Friars' by Richard Firth Green. A particularly useful look at fairy beliefs in the UK during and for a period after the conversion to Christianity and what the social factors of the human world may have done to influence various fairy beliefs across those times.

'Fairies, Fractious Women, and the Old Faith' by Regina Buccola. A look at various female figures associated with fairies across the UK and history. Useful for the deeper discussion of figures like Ann Jeffries who can be more difficult to study.

You'll notice there aren't many Irish specific books in there. Well, I haven't yet found a good solid historic text on Irish witchcraft, although I keep looking. For that area I comb through a wide array of Irish specific folklore, anthropology, and academic pagan texts and look at anecdotal material relating to cultural beliefs. My main resources for this right now would be Duchas. ie and Michael Fortune's YouTube videos, the Circle Stories page on Facebook, the Mythical Ireland site, and a collection of written texts.

Although I don't really draw on other modern practitioners there are a few who I enjoy reading or have found thought provoking or useful[1]. Not all of these are people who necessarily consider themselves witches and they aren't necessarily people I agree with 100%, but they are writers I think are worth considering. For that list we'd have:

'A Grimoire For Modern Cunningfolk' by Peter Paddon. Peter was a great guy and I enjoy his writing style and approach to the subject.

'Call of the Horned Piper' by Nigel Jackson. One of my favorites for modern traditional witchcraft, I found it really resonant.

'Essays From the Crossroads 2016 Collection' by Seo Helrune. So, I admit I'm a big fan of Seo Helrune. Love this book, love the blog (which I also recommend below). More focused on ancestor work than I am but very insightful and deliciously blunt and willing to confront hard truths.

'A Practical Guide to Irish Spirituality' by Lora O'Brien. Another of my favorite books, not witchcraft specific exactly but full of good material, much of which I find touches on actual practices.

'Traditional Witchcraft' by Gemma Gary. A really good resource on modern traditional witchcraft and also one with a really sound view of fairies

'Apocalyptic Witchcraft' by Peter Grey – complex and thought provoking.

'Deed Without a Name' by Lee Morgan – good overview of traditional witchcraft and an exceptional resource for the anecdotal material that is included.

Blogs

Via Hedera - a great blog looking at green witchcraft, animism and generally interesting witchcraft related subjects. Not exactly tradcraft but lots of great food for thought in related practices.

Seo Helrune – Norse and Anglo-Saxon focused. An invaluable resource for modern practices, especially relating to working with ancestors.

Lora O'Brien – Lora's blog covers an array of material relating to Irish paganism and the Good Folk.

* * *

So that covers all the main things I can think of. Some books and some blogs, some academic some personal, a mix of material. When it comes to my own practice, I look at these resources as well as the body of fairylore that we have, see what works and what doesn't through experience, and go from there.

Appendix B: Fiction

I often talk about my concerns with modern fiction and its portrayal of fairies, particularly the way they end up being humanized. While I understand why this happens and I can even appreciate it when reading it I see a lot of material from fiction that is clearly purely from an author's imagination making its way into modern pagan belief as if it were genuine folklore. Obviously, that's a concern to me on multiple levels. Given the focus here on bringing the Othercrowd back more fully into the human world and the way people look to fiction to understand folklore (consciously or not) I'm including a list of books I would recommend for people looking for good fairy-themed fiction. These are texts that generally hold much closer to the folklore than the bulk of what is on the market today and across the last 40 years or so.

Top Recommendations

These are the main books that I suggest people look for if they want good folkloric depictions of fairies in modern stories. No book is going to be 100% perfect but these are as close as I can think of, and they are also good stories:

'Lords and Ladies' by Terry Pratchett - a book in Pratchett's Disc World series I chose Lords and Ladies specifically because his view of the elves here is pretty spot on for how inhuman and inhumane they can be. To quote the book: *"... people didn't seem to be able to remember what it was like with the elves around. Life was certainly more interesting then, but usually because it was shorter. And it was more colorful, if you liked the color of blood."*
'Faery Sworn' by Ron C Neito - a very creative story but overall fairly true to the folklore. Some variance on what the Seelie and Unseelie courts are called, but does a great job of

including things like aversion to iron, viciousness, time slip between Fairy and earth, and etiquette. My only critique would be at the idea that there are only single beings in some of the categories we know from folklore, i.e. 'the kelpie' 'the nucklevee', but that's a fairly minor quibble.

'The Knowing' by Kevin Manwaring - hard to find at the moment, an excellent blend of older fairylore and the modern world. Based on the story of rev. Robert Kirk but imagining his descendants into our time, very accurate to older fairylore.

'The Call' by Peadar O'Guilin – a dystopian look at what might happen if the fey folk force their way back entirely on their own terms.

'Secret of the Kelpie' by Lari Don - a children's book, beautifully illustrated, and extremely true to folklore. A nice and necessary balance to many modern urban fantasy and young adult books that try to paint kelpies and other unseelie fairies as the good guys.

'Good Fairies of New York' by Martin Millar - a unique look at urban fairies, although I usually try to avoid stories of small winged fae this one is worth the read. I particularly liked the multicultural aspects the author brought into the city fairies.

'The Dubh Linn' series by Ruth Long – YA but lots of good folklore and an interesting take on the subject of Irish fairies in a modern urban setting.

'Jonathan Strange and Mr. Norrell' by Susanna Clark - complicated story about magicians in 19th century England but has a great deal of fairylore in it as well as accurate depictions of the Good People.

'Spiritwalk' by Charles de Lint - set in Canada, focused around a building, great mix of Celtic and North American fairylore.

Secondary Recommendations

These are also good books; however, they do venture further from the folklore and need to be read with a grain of salt or an existing grounding in the material:

'Modern Faery Tale' series by Holly Black - gets points for portraying fairies along mostly traditional lines, and as ruthless and often cruel; loses points for tons of YA tropes and some major plot holes.

'The SERRAted Edge' series and Bedlam Bard series by Mercedes Lackey - Primarily written in the 90's the SERRAted Edge series[2] looks at elves in modern America and includes a lot of folklore as well as some creative innovation, like the elves reacting to caffeine as if it were an addictive drug. The series is a bit dated at this point. The related Bedlam Bard series, which is set in the same universe and has some crossover, is also decent.

'Toby Daye' series by Seanan McGuire - modern fairies in America, reasonably close to folklore in many respects especially as regards politics in Fairy.

'The Elfhome series' by Wen Spencer - really interesting and creative look at an alternate reality where science has created an interdimensional gate that has accidentally shifted modern Pittsburgh into elfhome. Mixes tech with magic in fun ways, and uses Japanese folklore as a base, however it does take some creative liberties with that folklore that a Western audience may not fully recognize.

* * *

So, there you have it. That covers my main recommendations and some secondary recommendations. Generally speaking I think most urban fantasy, while my favorite genre, tends to fall into the secondary recommendations (I'd even include my own in that by the way) because in order to create the story liberties with the folklore have to be taken, especially where there are romantic themes or subthemes which is almost the entire genre.

It's often a safe bet to say if the fairies or a fairy in the book are main characters and even slightly relatable or sympathetic then liberties are being taken with the folklore (Faery Sworn is a notable and unusual exception).

End Notes

1   I am aware that there are many other books on the market in the genre of traditional witchcraft. Generally speaking, I have either read them already and they just didn't resonate with me, or I haven't been able to get a copy yet.

2   caveat I do not recommend the newest book in the series, 'Silence', which is co-written by Cody Martin. It ventures far from the rest of the series, and while the folklore isn't entirely inaccurate the book is not well written.

Bibliography

Acland, A., (2019) Tam Lin Balladry Retrieved from Tam-Lin.org

Bottrell, W., (1873) Traditions and Hearthside Stories of Cornwall, vol 2

Briggs, K., (1976) A Dictionary of Fairies

– (2003) The Anatomy of Puck: An Examination of Fairy Beliefs among Shakespeare's Contemporaries and Successors

Carmichael, A., (1900) Carmina Gadelica volume I

Child, F., (1882) The English and Scottish Popular Ballads

Crommond, W., (1903) The Records of Elgin, 1234–1800

Danaher, K., (1972) The Year in Ireland

Evans, E., (1957) Irish Folk Ways

Evans-Wentz, W., (1911) Fairy Faith in Celtic Countries

Geoghan, S., (2005) Gobnait: Woman of the Bees http://www.matrifocus.com/IMB05/ireland-gobnait.htm

Gibson, S., (2018) The Pleiades https://www.naic.edu/~gibson/pleiades/

Gillion, A., and Smith, J., (1953) Justiciary Cases

Halpin, D., (2018) The Pleiades and Beltane https://www.facebook.com/CircleStoriesDavidHalpin/photos/a.50810 6326204715/619216361760377/?type=3&permPage=1&hc_location=ufi

Harold Johnson and the Cursing Stones (2011) https://vimeo.com/16714531

Horne, J., (2018) Pleiades Sparkle On Winter Nights https://www.fayobserver.com/49a7eb0c-4d2a-5c97-afc9-b129ee59ba3b.html

Kamehamema Schools (2014) 'The rise of Makali'i marks a Hawaiian new year' Retrieved from https://www.ksbe.edu/imua/article/the-rise-of-makalii-marks-a-hawaiian-new-year/

Kelly, F., (2005) A Guide to Early Irish Law

Kramer, J., (2004) A Starry Calendar Part 1 https://www.lcasastronomy.org/articles/display.php?filename=a_starry_ calendar&category=observing

MacCoitir, N., (2006) Irish Wild Plants

Maclure, B., (2007) November is the Month of the Pleiades

– (2017) Pleiades Star Cluster; aka the seven sistersMaunder, E., (1906) Heliacal Risings and Settings of Stars

McCone, K., (1990) Pagan Past and Christian Present in Earl" Irish Literature

McNeill, F., (1956) The Silver Bough

Miller, J., (1877) Renfrewshire Witches

Murphy, A., (2017) Ancient Sites Dowth – Dubad

--- (2018) Ancient Astronomers of the Stone Age https:// mythicalireland.com/astronomy/ancient-astronomers-of-the-stone-age/

Ó hÓgáin, D., (1995) Irish Superstitions

Ó Súilleabháin, S., (1967) Nósanna agus Piseoga na nGeal

P. S. V. L. (2011) The Hidden Imbolc http://www.patheos.com/ blogs/pantheon/2011/02/the-hidden-imbolc/

Pitcairn, R., (1833) Ancient Criminal Trials in Scotland

Resnick, J., (2016) Grianan of Aileach in Ireland Aligns to Equinoxes https://www.spiritualsun.com/spiritual-sites/ grianan-of-aileach-in-ireland-aligns-to-equinoxes

Scott, W., (1827) Chronicles of Canongate

Scott, W., (1828) The Fair Maid of Perth

Seo Helrune (2018) 'Restoration Not Re-enchantment' retrieved from https://seohelrune.com/2018/10/29/restoration-not-reenchantment/

Sparavigna, A., (2008) The Pleiades: The celestial herd of ancient timekeepers

White, G., (2016) Star.Ships

Wilde, E., (1991) Irish Cures, Mystic Charms & Superstitions

Wimberly, C., (1928) Folklore in the English and Scottish Ballads

**MOON
BOOKS**

PAGANISM & SHAMANISM

What is Paganism? A religion, a spirituality, an alternative belief system, nature worship? You can find support for all these definitions (and many more) in dictionaries, encyclopaedias, and text books of religion, but subscribe to any one and the truth will evade you. Above all Paganism is a creative pursuit, an encounter with reality, an exploration of meaning and an expression of the soul. Druids, Heathens, Wiccans and others, all contribute their insights and literary riches to the Pagan tradition. Moon Books invites you to begin or to deepen your own encounter, right here, right now.

If you have enjoyed this book, why not tell other readers by posting a review on your preferred book site.

Medicine for the Soul
The Complete Book of Shamanic Healing
Ross Heaven
All you will ever need to know about shamanic healing and how to become your own shaman...
Paperback: 978-1-78099-419-2 ebook: 978-1-78099-420-8

Shaman Pathways – The Druid Shaman
Exploring the Celtic Otherworld
Danu Forest
A practical guide to Celtic shamanism with exercises and techniques as well as traditional lore for exploring the Celtic Otherworld.
Paperback: 978-1-78099-615-8 ebook: 978-1-78099-616-5

Traditional Witchcraft for the Woods and Forests
A Witch's Guide to the Woodland with Guided Meditations and Pathworking
Mélusine Draco
A Witch's guide to walking alone in the woods, with guided meditations and pathworking.
Paperback: 978-1-84694-803-9 ebook: 978-1-84694-804-6

Naming the Goddess
Trevor Greenfield
Naming the Goddess is written by over eighty adherents and scholars of Goddess and Goddess Spirituality.
Paperback: 978-1-78279-476-9 ebook: 978-1-78279-475-2

Shapeshifting into Higher Consciousness
Heal and Transform Yourself and Our World with Ancient
Shamanic and Modern Methods
Llyn Roberts
Ancient and modern methods that you can use every day to
transform yourself and make a positive difference in the world.
Paperback: 978-1-84694-843-5 ebook: 978-1-84694-844-2

Readers of ebooks can buy or view any of these bestsellers by
clicking on the live link in the title. Most titles are published in
paperback and as an ebook. Paperbacks are available in traditional
bookshops. Both print and ebook formats are available online.

Find more titles and sign up to our readers' newsletter at
http://www.johnhuntpublishing.com/paganism
Follow us on Facebook at https://www.facebook.com/MoonBooks
and Twitter at https://twitter.com/MoonBooksJHP